Dash panels
Copper tubing
fuel tank ?
hollow tubing
streamline "u"
L channel
thin rod
Staybrite
Kan ty's 8200
Rub 'n' Buff (Brass)
Prop
Pitot cock ———— (Alemite)
Rheostat   Shop
Dirigible
Plumbing supply brass rng's
Winch handles

Metalwork
for
Craftsmen
A Step by Step Guide
with 55 Projects

formerly titled: Art Metalwork

EMIL F. KRONQUIST

DOVER PUBLICATIONS, INC.
NEW YORK

Published in Canada by General Publishing Company, Ltd., 30 Lesmill Road, Don Mills, Toronto, Ontario.
Published in the United Kingdom by Constable and Company, Ltd., 10 Orange Street, London WC 2.

This Dover edition, first published in 1972, is a republication of the work originally published by McGraw-Hill Book Co., Inc., in 1942 under the title *Art Metalwork*. The main text is complete and unabridged, but the brief and outdated lists of dealers and books of interest to craftworkers in metal have been omitted.

Twenty-eight illustrations have been added to this edition.

International Standard Book Number: 0-486-22789-8
Library of Congress Catalog Card Number: 78-160856

Manufactured in the United States of America
Dover Publications, Inc.
180 Varick Street
New York, N. Y. 10014

PREFACE

The constructive use of leisure time is a necessary balance for a life of work, and planning for leisure hours is fast becoming a fundamental factor in our educational practices. To contrive a quiet place in heart and mind, to widen a life until it spreads beyond all human fear and fever, that is to touch the sources of eternal peace.

New interests are vital. Hobbies have multitudinous possibilities. The real satisfaction in life comes as one reaches out and acquires a discriminating appreciation for that which is fine, that which is real, and that which is beautiful. The ability to disinguish between a genuine etching and a reproduction, a beautiful handbound book and a cheap edition, a pure linen cloth and a substitute, a piece of hand-chased silver and a stamping, together with a taste for pleasingly applied colors—these are the things that bring lasting satisfaction to the intelligent adult.

It has been said that "higher recreation" is a part of "higher education." In planning for higher recreation, we should include the arts and crafts and the pursuit of cultural skills. For many years it has been my privilege to teach metalcraft to classes of men and women—young, middle-aged, and old. One of my greatest thrills as an instructor has come when I have been able to see a student's project carried to a successful conclusion through his persistent efforts. No one can buy the peace and pride that come from a successful accomplishment. Nor can one purchase the glow that goes into the making of a hand-wrought gift for a cherished friend.

In this age of specialization, we need to concentrate our avocational interests upon something that has enough intrinsic worth to make the hard work and the sacrifice worth the time and effort.

The novice in art metal, as in other endeavors, is often impatient in his desire to produce his "masterpiece" and to reach perfection in too short a time and with too little effort. He forgets that nothing can be, nor ever has been, accomplished in the field of art without practice and determination. This is true, likewise, in the fields of industry and commerce.

Age has nothing to do with one's ability to master a craft. One often hears excuses for ineffectualness on the grounds that "an old dog cannot be taught new tricks." In my own clasess of adult students, I have seen that theory exploded many times. My personal experience puts me in perfect agreement with Professor Edward Thorndike when he says that, "With determination and application one can learn anything one wants to at any time of life."

One of the basic psychological needs of the individual is that of success. In hobbies, as in life work, the sooner the individual learns to concentrate on the things he can influence, the sooner his efforts cease to be subjected to frustration. Inasmuch as the possibilities in designing are limited by the extent of the craftsman's knowledge of the medium in which he intends to work, this aggregation of projects has been compiled to help him.

The approach is from the craftworker's point of view with descriptions of simple workshop methods that the author has found to be practicable, both commercially and in teaching.

Appreciating the fact that the average craftworker acquires a more comprehensive understanding through the graphic language, five hundred work sketches have been used to describe the procedures. The reading matter has been reduced to the minimum and includes only such information as is pertinent to the immediate work at hand.

EMIL F. KRONQUIST.

CONTENTS

INTRODUCTION

This book goes out from the hand and heart of a master crafts-man to his classroom comrades. He has served as mentor and guide to young people in all types of secondary institutions. His young friends have always worthily employed the tools and materials. Their skill and productive achievement have come to constitute what teachers call perfect integration.

The Swedish artist who writes this book first lived it in our high schools—both traditional and vocational. His happy years in Danish schools and shops were matured by years of cultural and vocational labor in England. Three decades of Milwaukee commercial crafts-manship and daily companionship with budding young craftsmen in our schools have naturally led to the clear, concise expositions found in these pages. No timorous young adventurer into the mysteries of beautiful old craftsmanship will here fail of his sure help.

MILTON C. POTTER,
Superintendent of Schools,
Milwaukee, Wisconsin.

To Dr. Robert Laurence Cooley

*the great schoolmaster—whose pioneering vision
and dynamic spirit have done so much to open up
the full vista of possibilities for genuine service to
the youth of America, and whose foresight has
been so largely responsible for the forward
look in adult education.*

*For his never-failing belief in those educational
ideals which help to change people ethically and
aesthetically; for his understanding and knowledge
of their changing needs; and for his sympathetic
interest in the crafts as an avocational outlet,
this book is gratefully dedicated.*

ROBERT L. COOLEY
EDUCATOR   FRIEND

(Modeled in low relief and finished in bronze by EMIL F. KRONQUIST.)

LABOR — REWARD

There is a perennial nobleness, and even sacredness, in work. Were he never so benighted, forgetful of his high calling, there is always hope in a man that actually and earnestly works; in idleness alone is there despair.—A man perfects himself by working, foul jungles are cleared away, fair seedfields rise instead, and stately cities.—Consider how, even in the meanest sorts of labor, the whole soul of a man is composed into a kind of real harmony, the instant he sets himself to work.—Blessed is he who has found his work; let him ask no other blessedness. He has a work, a life purpose; he has found it, and will follow it.—Labor is life: From the inmost heart of the worker rises his God given force, the sacred celestial life essence breathed into him by Almighty God; from his inmost heart awakens him to all nobleness—to all knowledge, "self-knowledge" and much else, so soon as work fitly begins.—Doubt, of whatever kind, can be ended by action alone.

—THOMAS CARLYLE (1795–1881).

TOOLS AND METALWORKING PROCESSES

TOOLS AND EQUIPMENT

Some of the common tools used by the metal craftworker are shown on the opposite page; others may be added as the need arises. Hammers and stakes are the most important tools and demand more attention and care than all others. The hammers should be of steel; the faces should be free from nicks and blemishes. The planishing hammers should have a mirror finish.

Tools Shown in Illustrations

1. Ball-peen hammer.
2. Sinking or plate hammer.
3. Raising hammer.
4. Planishing hammer.
5. Chasing hammer, also used for planishing.
6. Rawhide mallet.
7. Ball or mushroom stake.
8. Raising stake.
9. Bick iron stake.
10. Loose head for bick iron.
11. Bottom stake.
12. Jeweler's saw.
13. Hack saw.
14. Shears or snips.
15. Try square.
16. Cutting pliers.
17. Flatnose pliers.
18. Hand drill.
19. Bunsen burner.
20. Dividers.
21. Bench vise.

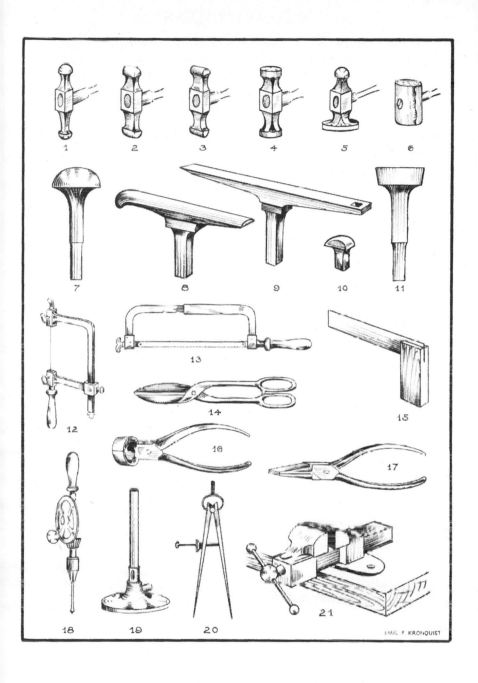

1 2 3 4 5 6

7 8 9 10 11

12 13 15

14

16 17

18 19 20 21

EMIL F. KRONQUIST

CUTTING OF STOCK

The cutting of stock for the execution of a job sometimes requires a good deal of preparatory work, such as the making of patterns or templates, the selecting of materials and gauges of metal to be used, and figuring the length of wire. This preparation is made in order to have the least possible waste of material.

Sometimes the stock must be cut with a slight allowance for cleaning off. This waste margin, of course, should not be too wide. Just sufficient metal should be left so that the raw cutting edge can be filed smooth.

Cutting with Shears

For general work a pair of straight shears 12 inches long is most useful (Fig. 1). For cutting heavier gauge metal the shears can be fastened in the vise, as shown in Fig. 2. The metal is cut with greater ease when the shears are held at a slight angle, as shown in Fig. 3.

Cutting with Hack Saw

The hack saw is used for cutting wire rods or tubing (Fig. 4). The blade is made of hard steel and breaks easily when given a sudden jerk or twist. A saw blade with 32 teeth per inch is best suited for craftwork and should be replaced whenever it becomes dull. A pair of false jaws for the vise (Fig. 7) should be used to protect the material from unnecessary marring. Most hack saws are made so that the blade can be swiveled at right angles or upside down.

Cutting with Jeweler's Saw

This is one of the most useful tools of the craftworker. Although it is made in many depths, a 5-inch saw is recommended. The blades are purchased in bundles, by the gross, or by the dozen lot; for general work a No. 2 blade is best. The blade is placed in the frame with the teeth pointing toward the handle; it works on the down stroke (Fig. 5).

Other methods of cutting heavy gauge metal with a chisel, hammer, and saw are shown in Figs. 6, 8, and 9.

4

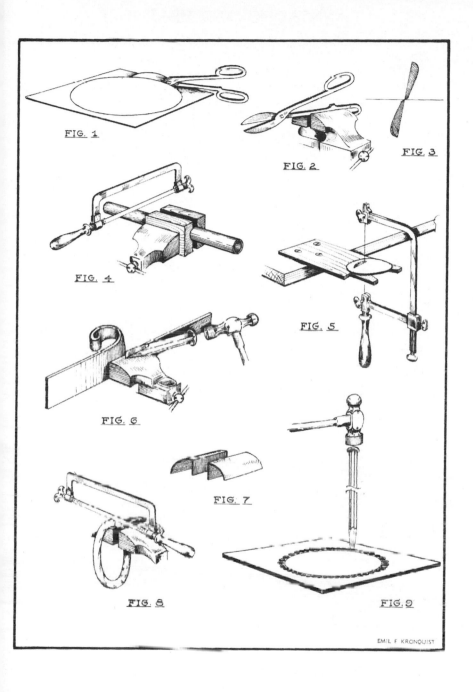

FIG. 1

FIG. 2

FIG. 3

FIG. 4

FIG. 5

FIG. 6

FIG. 7

FIG. 8

FIG. 9

EMIL F KRONQUIST

ANNEALING AND HEATING

Annealing is the name given to the process of softening metal by means of heating.

During the working and shaping, metal becomes hard, either by compression or by tension, and annealing has to be resorted to before any further shaping can be done. Annealing reduces the hardness and removes the strains that have been induced in the material by some previous treatment.

Without annealing, it would be impossible for the craftsman to fashion some pieces of work; therefore, heating becomes a matter of extreme importance.

Annealing with a Torch

Adjust the air and the gas until a blue flame appears. Move the flame slowly over the entire metal surface until it is uniformly red (Fig. 1).

Annealing Small Pieces over a Bunsen Burner

Hold the metal at a corner with a pair of pliers (Fig. 2). The point of the inner air cone of the flame is the hottest (Fig. 3).

Annealing with a Mouth Blowpipe and Alcohol Lamp

A little practice is required in order to produce an even blue flame (Fig. 4).

Annealing of Wire

Coil the wire in a tight bundle; move a soft flame to and fro over it until it becomes red.

Annealing Aluminum

Move the flame slowly over the surface; touch the metal with a stick of wood (match). If the metal scorches the wood, it is hot enough. Experiment with a scrap of aluminum.

Softening of Pewter

Move a soft flame (no air) over the metal surface; moisten a finger and touch the metal at different spots, listening for a sizzling of the moisture.

Precautions

Overheating may cause the metal to melt.
Spotty heating should be avoided.
Alloyed metals should not be picked up while they are red hot.
Small size wire cannot be annealed safely in single strands.
Aluminum stays white; no pickling is necessary.

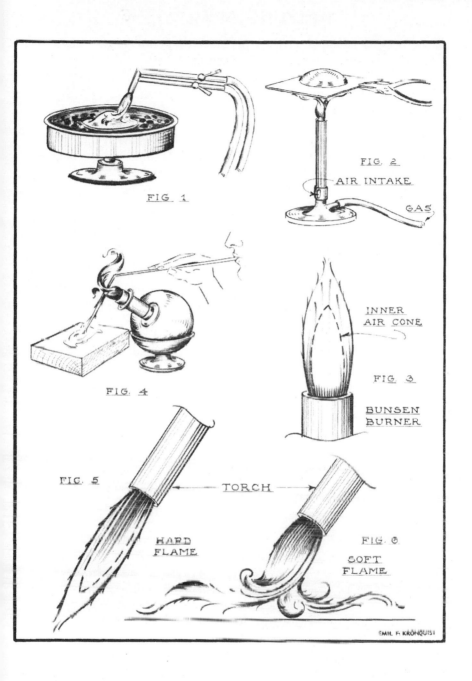

FIG. 1

FIG. 2
AIR INTAKE
GAS

FIG. 4

INNER
AIR CONE
FIG. 3
BUNSEN
BURNER

FIG. 5
TORCH
HARD
FLAME

FIG. 6
SOFT
FLAME

EMIL F. KRONQUIST

PICKLING OF METALS

Pickling is the term used by metalworkers when an object is plunged, dipped, suspended, or boiled in some kind of acid solution for the purpose of removing or dissolving the oxide or scale formed on the metal in the process of annealing.

The pickling of metals is an essential part of the work of the craftsman. It would be difficult to see any of the blows of the hammer or to do any kind of marking on the surface of the metal if the oxide were not removed. Scrubbing with an abrasive, such as kitchen cleanser or pumice powder, would take too long and would not accomplish what acid does in a couple of minutes.

Iron tools, such as pliers, tongs, and tweezers, must be kept out of the acid.

Pickling Solution for Copper, Brass, and Silver

To 1 gallon of cold water, add about 6 ounces of commercial sulphuric acid (Fig. 1) and stir with a stick of wood. (Water should *never* be added to sulphuric acid, nor should sulphuric acid be added to boiling water, because steam is generated which causes a small explosion and may result in serious acid burns.)

Procedure to Be Followed When Pickling

1. Pick up the annealed metal with the pickup tongs (Fig. 3) or a pair of pliers.
2. Step back an arm's length and drop the metal, while hot, into the pickling bath.
3. Wait a minute or two for the oxide to dissolve, then pick it up with a stick of wood (Fig. 2). Rinse the metal thoroughly in running water.
4. Dry the metal with a clean rag or dry it in hardwood sawdust (Fig. 5).

Alloyed metals, such as brass, bronze, and nickel silver should be allowed to cool slightly before being thrown into the acid solution.

A hot pickling solution will dissolve the oxide and clean the metal quicker than a cold solution; it will also dissolve a borax flux (Fig. 4).

Sterling silver becomes pure white after boiling. The pickling solution dissolves the extracted deposit of oxide formed in the process of heating and leaves a coating of fine silver on the surface.

8

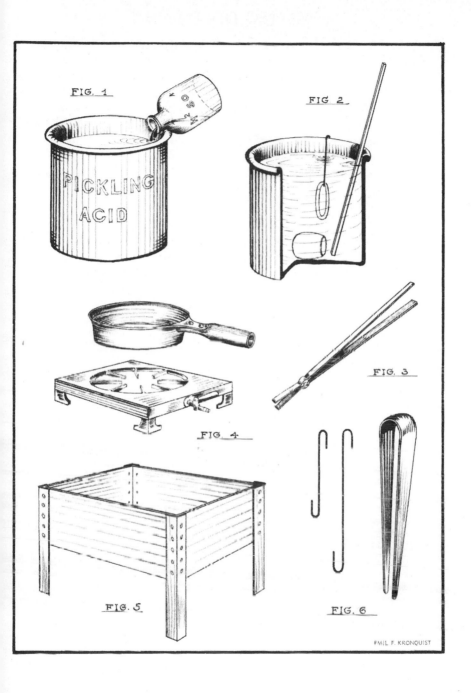

FIG. 1

FIG 2

PICKLING
ACID

FIG. 3

FIG. 4

FIG. 5

FIG. 6

EMIL F. KRONQUIST

SHALLOW HOLLOWING

Several methods may be employed in hammering up a shallow piece of work. It is best to be guided by the shape of the design in choosing the method of execution and also by the available equipment. The most elementary way of making a small bowl is shown in successive steps on the opposite page. A ball-peen or hollowing hammer is used; also, a block of wood having a hollow depression on the end grain side. The metal disk is hammered along the outer edge first and continuing inward toward the center, the metal being stretched down into the hollow depression in the wood. The consequent thinning of the metal naturally limits the depth.

Procedure to Be Followed in Making

1. Cut the circular metal disk.
2. Draw a few concentric circles for guide lines.
3. Begin hammering along the outer edge, continuing in circular fashion until the center is reached. Avoid striking the edge of the metal (Fig. 1).
4. Anneal the metal. Pickle, if necessary.
5. Repeat the hammering until the desired depth has been reached. Anneal between each beating (Figs. 2, 3, 4, and 5).
6. Place the bowl on a mushroom stake and smooth the surface with a mallet (Fig. 6).
7. Anneal and clean the metal; then planish the entire surface, starting in the center (Fig. 7). (See *Planishing*.)
8. Trim the edge with a pair of shears (Fig. 8).
9. Flatten the bottom (Fig. 9).
10. True the bottom, making a slight cove (Fig. 10).
11. Finish the edge to any desired design (Fig. 11).

In estimating, the diameter of the metal disk needed for hollowing is approximately the largest diameter of the design, plus the height. This, however, varies with the material used and how the individual works.

Folds in the metal will lead to subsequent cracking.

A wavy top edge should be corrected as the work proceeds.

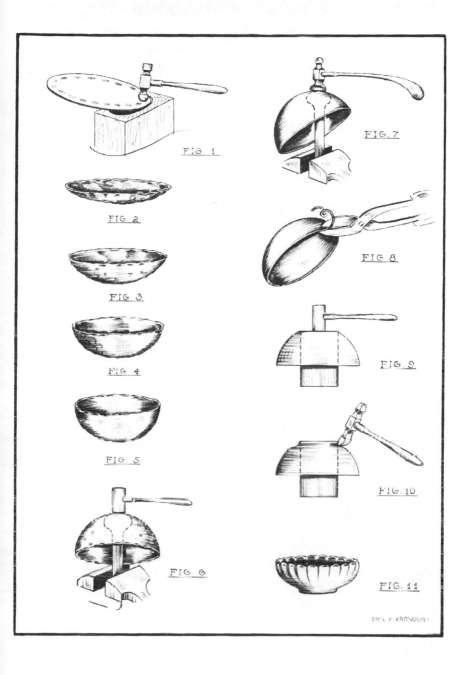

FIG. 1

FIG. 2

FIG. 3

FIG. 4

FIG. 5

FIG. 6

FIG. 7

FIG. 8

FIG. 9

FIG. 10

FIG. 11

EMIL F. KRONQUIST

SHALLOW RAISING WITH WEDGE MALLET

This method of raising a shallow vessel differs from the hollowing process in that the metal disk is worked from the outside. It is a contracting process, rather than a stretching process. The metal disk may be crimped as shown in Fig. 1 before the actual raising is started, but it is not necessary.

The raising is done by placing the disk on a T stake as shown, or a mushroom stake may be used, then contracting the metal with a wedge-shaped mallet, working in circles from the center to the edge. This method of shaping a piece of work does not thin the metal as hollowing does. It is the professional way of executing a first-class job.

Procedure to Be Followed in Making

1. Cut the circular disk.
2. Draw a few concentric circles with a pencil compass for guide lines.
3. Place the metal disk on a stake, as shown in Fig. 2, and begin raising it with a wedge-shaped mallet. When the edge has been reached, the work will look as in Fig. 3.
4. Anneal the metal; pickle, if necessary.
5. Draw the guide lines and repeat the raising until the desired depth has been reached (Figs. 4, 5, and 6). The metal must be annealed after each raising.
6. Trim the edge with a pair of shears, as shown in Fig. 7.
7. Planish the work on a suitable shaped mushroom stake to remove all blemishes. Repeat, if necessary.
8. Flatten the bottom with a mallet (Fig. 8).
9. True up the bottom by making a shallow cove (Fig. 9).
10. Finish the edge to any desired shape.

The approximate diameter of the disk required is the largest diameter of the design, plus the over-all height.

The blows of the mallet should be delivered evenly.

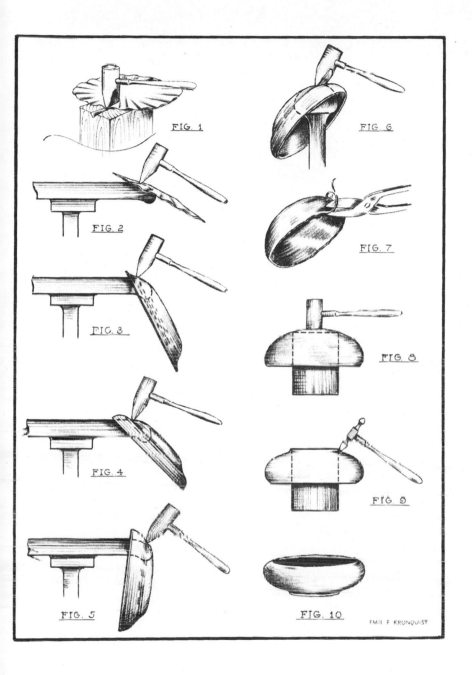

FIG. 1

FIG. 2

FIG. 3

FIG. 4

FIG. 5

FIG. 6

FIG. 7

FIG. 8

FIG. 9

FIG. 10

EMIL F KRONQUIST

RAISING

Raising is the process of shaping a hollow vessel from a flat disk of sheet metal by using hammers and mallets and stakes (Figs. 1 and 2). The craftsmen of old were masters of the art of raising and it may still be regarded as a basic process.

Great height can be attained by careful and systematic hammering and annealing. The process differs from hollow and shallow raising in that the metal is worked almost entirely on the outside— a contracting operation, so to speak.

Procedure to Be Followed in Raising (Typical Example)

1. Cut a metal disk, the diameter of which should be approximately "the largest diameter plus the greatest height" of the design, 7 inches (Fig. 3).
2. Anneal the metal.
3. The raising may be started in either one of two ways:
   a. Doming up a shallow bowl (Fig. 4).
   b. Crimping the disk, as shown in Fig. 5. This may be done on a block of wood.
4. Anneal and pickle the metal.
5. Draw a circle on the outside of the bowl equal in diameter to that of the bottom of the design.
6. Place the work on the raising stake, as shown in Figs. 6 and 7, and begin hammering, going round and round, crowding a little metal upward toward the edge by each blow of the hammer. It is important to hold the metal against the nose of the stake in such a way that the hammer blow lands just above the point of contact. On the last round, along the edge, use a wood mallet.
7. Anneal and pickle the metal.

From this point on, it is a repetition of the processes described in Steps 6 and 7. The blows of the raising hammer must fall squarely on the metal and the work must be moved back on the stake as the edge is approached (Fig. 8).

Pencil guide lines must be described on the work at the beginning of each course of hammering.

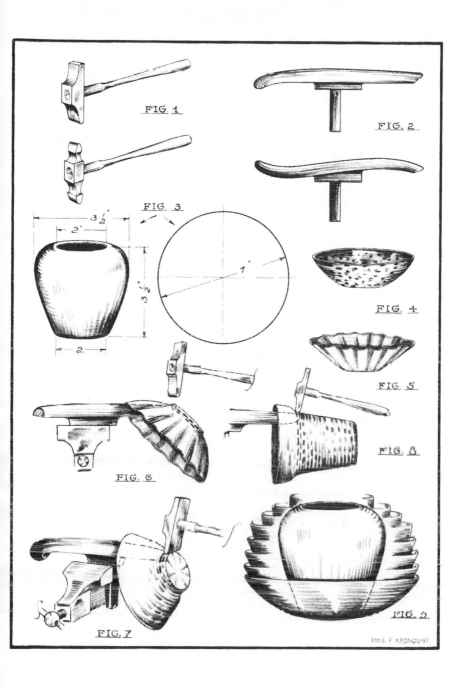

FIG. 1

FIG. 2

FIG. 3

FIG. 4

FIG. 5

FIG. 6

FIG. 8

FIG. 7

FIG. 9

EMIL F. KRONQUIST

PLANISHING

Planishing is the process of making a metallic surface smooth by hammering lightly and producing, one might say, a texture. Only tools with a mirror-polished working surface should be used. Often the process is repeated several times before all blemishes and bruises from previous hammering have disappeared. To distribute the blows of the hammer evenly requires much patient practice. The arm should be kept close to the body and a wrist motion used in delivering the light blows of the hammer.

A mirror finish on a planishing hammer may be produced in the following manner:

1. Tack a sheet of emery cloth, No. 180 grit, on a board with four small nails, squirt plenty of oil on the emery, and rub back and forth until all rough marks have disappeared.
2. Tack a sheet of emery cloth, No. 280 grit, on another board, oil it, and rub the hammer back and forth until all the scratches produced by the coarser grit have disappeared.
3. Tack on third board a sheet of emery cloth, No. 360 grit, oil and rub as before.   The steel is now ready for the final polish.
4. Tack a sheet of crocus cloth (rouge cloth) on a board, squirt plenty of oil on it, and rub the hammer until it shines like a mirror.

This polishing equipment should be wrapped up and stored for future use.

Procedure to Be Followed in Planishing

1. Clean the metal so that it is free from grease and oxides.
2. Select a stake or iron that has a curvature as near to that of the work as possible (Fig. 1).
3. Select a hammer of suitable weight and shape (Fig. 2).
4. Place the work on the stake.
5. Begin planishing. The fall of the hammer should be square on the work at the point of contact (Fig. 3).

The hammer blows should fall evenly, the work being rotated or moved so that no two blows fall in the same place.

Planishing should not alter the shape of the work; it should true it, close the granular texture, and remove irregularities from the surface. Planishing stretches the work slightly. Concentric pencil circles should be described on circular work to act as guide lines. Planishing may be repeated several times.

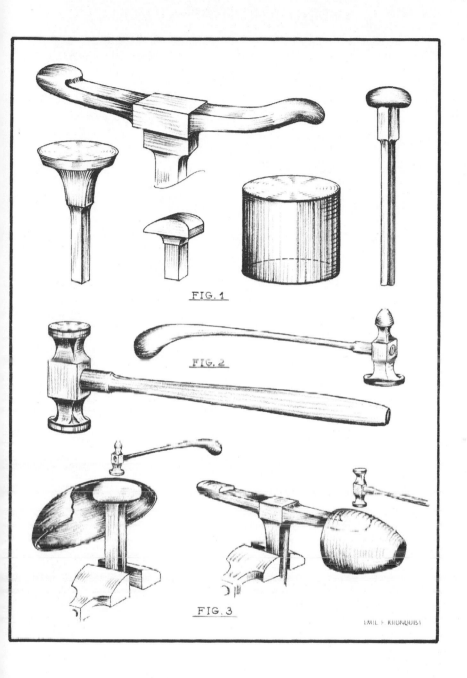

FIG. 1

FIG. 2

FIG. 3

EMIL F. RHONQUIST

BENDING AND SHAPING METAL

Bending and shaping sheet metal and wire often must be done over specially prepared blocks of wood or iron. Devices called "jigs" sometimes are made when duplicate pieces have to be formed. Hand pressure should be employed whenever possible and, as a rule, is sufficient, at least when handling the lighter gauges of metal. A mallet or hammer is necessary when dealing with heavy-gauge metal or bar stock.

Metal should be annealed before any bending is attempted, and sometimes the metal must be reannealed before the final shape is reached.

Methods of Bending and Shaping Metal

1. Squeeze the metal between two pieces of wood or metal (Figs. 1 and 2).
2. Bend over specially prepared forms or around pieces of steel. Due allowance should be made for spring back when wire is bent (Fig. 3).
3. Shape with bending jigs such as are shown in Figs. 5 and 6. Scrolls should be started as shown in Fig. 4 and may be finished entirely with a hammer and various stakes.
4. Score with blunt chisel or chasing tool to secure a sharp bend. The tool must be blunt and the angle of the bevel should be approximately ninety degrees (Figs. 7 and 8). This scoring process requires considerable practice before it can be executed accurately.
5. Shape with a sheet-metalworker's brake.

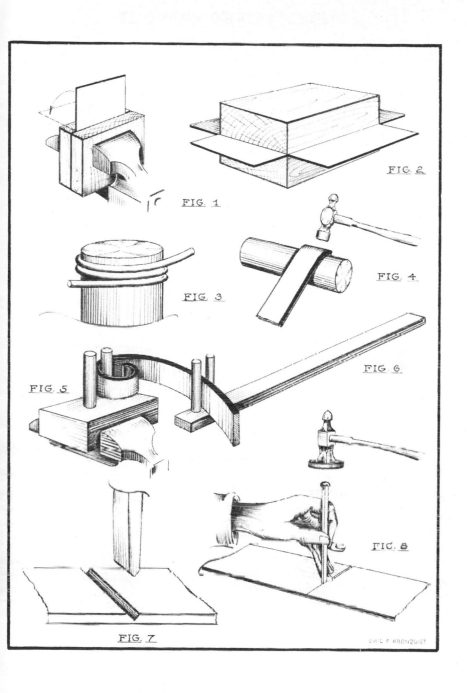

FIG. 1

FIG. 2

FIG. 3

FIG. 4

FIG. 5

FIG. 6

FIG. 7

FIG. 8

EMIL F. HRONQUIST

LEVELING AND TRUING UP

In order to make and keep a piece of work level and true in the course of its shaping processes, it is necessary to apply simple tests from time to time. Truing, testing, and correcting should be considered a part of the work, equal in importance to any of the operations in the making. Irregularity of hammering, different weights of the blow of the hammer, and lack of guide lines all contribute to the unevenness of the work.

Procedure to Be Followed in Leveling a Vessel (Fig. 7)

1. Hold the work at arm's length and sight for unevenness.
2. Clip off roughly any extreme high spot.
3. Adjust the needle of the surface gauge (Fig. 7) to the height required and lock the different adjustment nuts.
4. Hold the work lightly but firmly with one hand and move the gauge with the other so that the needle scratches a line to indicate how much of the metal should be removed.
5. Clip or file to the line.

Many improvised methods can be used in place of a surface gauge, such as a pencil held firmly on a block of wood (Fig. 8) or a compass or divider held the same way (Fig. 9).

Small size annealed wire and tubing are straightened by being rolled between two flat surface irons (Fig. 5). Another method is by pulling: one end is held in the vise and the other in a pair of pliers, then stretched.

A wire ring or molding usually has to be trued and fitted in two directions, flat and circular. The flatting is done on a surface plate with a mallet (Fig. 6). The rounding is done on a stake by rotating the work slowly while it is being struck lightly with a rawhide mallet.

FIG. 1

FIG. 2

FIG. 3

FIG. 4

FIG. 5

FIG. 6

FIG. 7

FIG. 8

FIG. 9

EMIL F. KRONQUIST

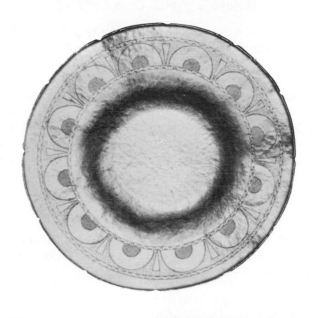

WIRING AND CLAMPING

A great deal of ingenuity is sometimes required to scheme out methods of holding pieces of metal together while they are being soldered.

Annealed iron wire is most generally used for this purpose. The nature of the job naturally determines what gauge of wire should be used; Nos. 18, 22, and 28 are good sizes to have on hand and they can always be doubled up and twisted if any heavier wire is wanted. Annealed iron wire is very cheap and can be purchased from hardware dealers. It is one of the very few things still sold by the very old unit of weight, "stone," which is about 14 pounds.

There are times when it is well to protect the edges of the work, especially when soldering pewter, with small pieces of metal or even with heavy manila paper, as shown in Fig. 1.

Ordinary wood clothespins are handy fastening devices to use when soft soldering. Dip them in water before using (Fig. 7).

Cotter pins are useful clamps for holding pieces together when hard soldering (Fig. 7).

Procedure for Tying Up a Cylinder for Hard Soldering (Fig. 2)

1. Fit the joint carefully.
2. Stretch the iron wire, clinch one end of the wire in a vise, grip the other with a pair of pliers, and pull hard.
3. Loop the wire in two places and bend it around the cylinder; twist the ends.
4. Insert two pieces of heavier wire near the joint for the purpose of elevating the binding wire slightly above the metal surface.
5. Tighten the wire around the cylinder by twisting the four loops.

Other methods are shown in Figs. 3, 4, 5, and 6.

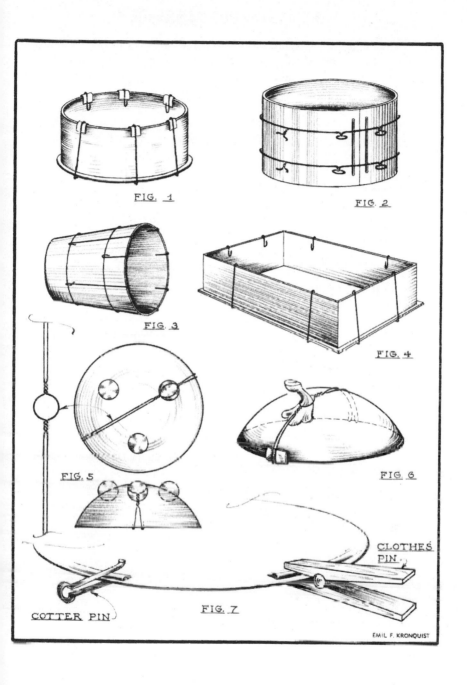

FIG. 1

FIG. 2

FIG. 3

FIG. 4

FIG. 5

FIG. 6

CLOTHES
PIN

COTTER PIN

FIG. 7

EMIL F. KRONQUIST

WIRE AND TUBE MAKING

Wire of any kind may be reduced in size by being pulled through the holes in a drawplate with a pair of tongs (Fig. 1). The drawplate is a steel plate with a series of holes, graduated in size (Fig. 2). These holes may be of any shape, such as round, half round, square, or any special design.

Tubing is formed with the same tools but started from a strip of metal. (This does not refer to seamless tubing, which is made from a different process.)

The holes in a drawplate are all tapered, as shown in Fig. 3. The wire must be filed to a point so that it can be gripped with the tongs. The pull should be steady, not jerky. A drop of oil applied to wire makes pulling a little easier. If a great reduction in the size of the wire is wanted, then it is well to anneal from time to time.

Procedure to Be Followed in Making a Piece of Tubing

1. Clip a strip of metal, $5\!/\!16$ inch wide, No. 24 gauge, and point one end (Fig. 4).
2. Hammer or bend the strip into the shape of a gutter (Fig. 5).
3. Fasten the drawplate in the bench vise. Protect the plate by using false jaws in the vise.
4. Stick the pointed end of the metal strip in the largest hole in the drawplate. Grip it with the tongs and pull it through the hole.
5. Repeat the operation, pulling the metal through successive holes until the desired size is obtained.

A tube may be made with a definite size hole by inserting a steel wire (piano wire) in the tube and drawing the tube around this wire. Pull the steel wire out by reversing the plate in the vise and stick the steel wire through a hole of its size and pull (Fig. 7).

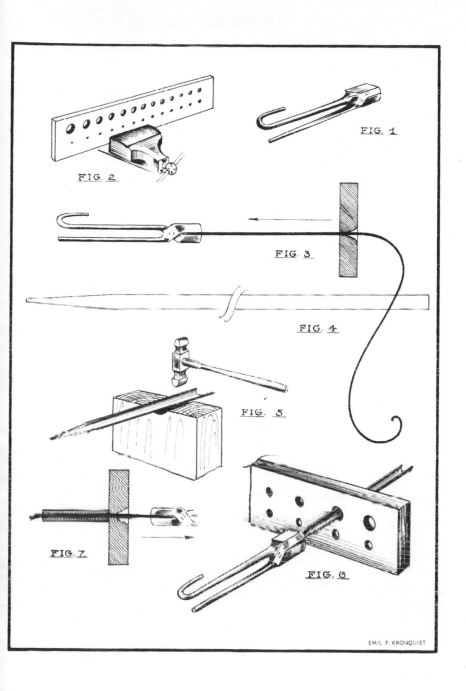

FIG. 1

FIG. 2

FIG. 3

FIG. 4

FIG. 5

FIG. 7

FIG. 6

EMIL F. KRONQUIST

TINNING AND CLEANING A SOLDERING BIT

A clean hot soldering bit is important for successful soldering. Oxides form on the bit in the process of heating and these must be removed. The soldering copper, or bit, as it is commonly called, is made in many sizes and different shapes. A large bit will retain the heat longer than a small one.

The flux used for cleaning and tinning is zinc chloride (muriatic acid with zinc added). A handier way is to have a small jar of "soldering salt" and to make up a little flux as it is needed by adding water to the salt.

Tools Needed

Soldering copper (Figs. 1, 2, and 3).
Heating furnace (Fig. 4). An ordinary gas plate will do.
Flux (Fig. 5).
Tin or soft solder (Figs. 6 and 8).
Old file.
Sal ammoniac (Fig. 7).

Procedure to Be Followed

1. Heat the bit to a very dull red.
2. Dip the point of the bit in the flux for an instant (Fig. 5).
3. Apply a small amount of solder to the point of the hot bit (Fig. 6).
4. Dip it again in the flux.

The soldering bit will appear bright and shiny white on the tip after this tinning and dipping in the flux.

Soldering bits can also be cleaned and tinned by rubbing the point on a piece of sal ammoniac where a piece of solder has been placed (Fig. 7).

If the bit has been overheated, it may be necessary to use an old file to remove the scale.

Solder in wire form, $\frac{1}{16}$ inch in diameter, is most suitable for art metalwork (Fig. 8).

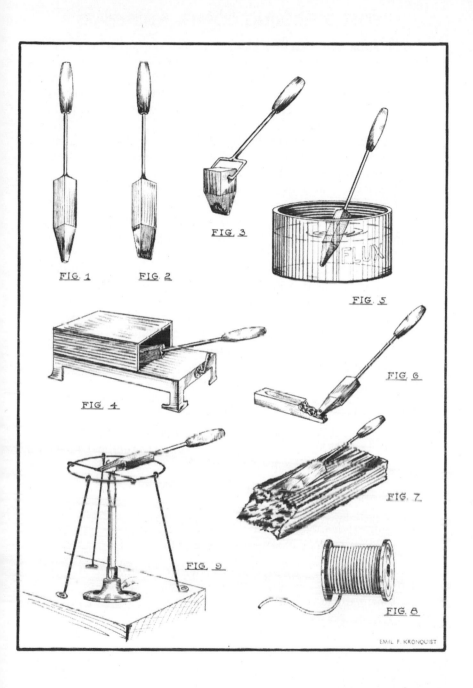

FIG. 1

FIG. 2

FIG. 3

FIG. 5

FIG. 4

FIG. 6

FIG. 7

FIG. 9

FIG. 8

EMIL F. KRONQUIST

SOFT SOLDERING COPPER AND BRASS

"Soft soldering" is the name given to a process of soldering where only a low degree of temperature is needed and the metal is never brought to a red heat as in "hard soldering." It is a much used process for simple and elementary work and comparatively cheap. There is not much strength in a soft-soldered joint and it is rarely used in advanced work, never on silver.

Soft solder is a combination, or alloy, of tin and lead. Sometimes bismuth and cadmium are added to lower the melting temperature. It can be purchased in bar or wire form. The handiest and most useful size for craftworkers is the 50-50 wire solder, $\frac{1}{16}$ inch in diameter. (The 50-50 means half lead and half tin.)

When metal is heated, it becomes oxidized, and it is impossible to solder on an oxidized surface; a "flux," therefore, must be used. Zinc chloride (muriatic acid with zinc added) is a good flux to use, but "soldering salt" can be bought anywhere and it is handier to make up a little as it is needed. The flux prevents oxidation of the metal while it is being moderately heated.

Members to be united by soldering must be well fitted and clean and often held together with wires or clamps. There are many ways in which heat can be applied to the work—by blow torch, mouth blowpipe, Bunsen burner, alcohol lamp, ordinary gas stove, or soldering bit.

Procedure to Be Followed (Typical Job)

1. Apply the flux to the joint, using a small cheap brush (Fig. 1).
2. Heat the work until the flux boils. Apply the heat in such a way that both members become equally hot. It may be necessary to invert the flame occasionally (Figs. 2 and 3).
3. Swab the joint with flux a second time.
4. Apply the heat again. Shortly after the boiling of the flux the joint should be touched quickly with the wire solder, as shown in Fig. 2. Small pieces of solder may be placed along the joint, as shown in Fig. 3.
5. Rinse in water and remove all wires.

Other methods are shown in Figs. 4, 5, and 6.

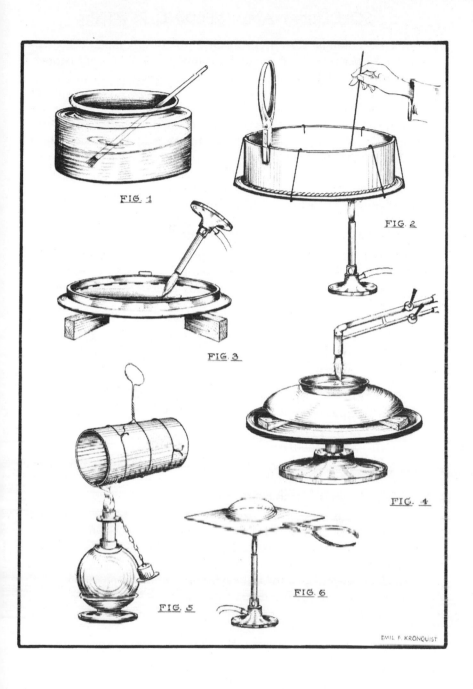

FIG. 1

FIG. 2

FIG. 3

FIG. 4

FIG. 5

FIG. 6

EMIL F. KRONQUIST

SOLDERING AND WELDING PEWTER

A good grade of pewter, also called "Britannia metal," is composed of 92 per cent tin, 6 per cent antimony, and 2 per cent copper. It is a soft metal. It is easy to work and retains its beautiful luster for a long time with very little attention. The metal may be either soldered or fused into a permanent union. Great care must be exercised in the application of heat because of the low melting temperature of the metal. When soldering, strong acid fluxes should be avoided because of their harmful effect in pitting the surface of the metal.

An excellent flux for pewter is made by adding 10 drops of hydrochloric acid to 1 ounce of glycerine.

Procedure to Be Followed in Soldering Pewter

1. Apply the flux to the prepared joint with a small brush.
2. Cut small pieces of wire solder, 50-50, of sizes suitable for the work at hand. (The wire solder may be flattened like a ribbon by hammering.)
3. Place the solder along the joint. Use a pair of tweezers.
4. Hold the work over the flame (Fig. 1) or apply the flame to the work (Figs. 2 and 3). Move it slowly back and forth and watch closely for the solder to melt.

Extra easy-flowing solder, for use in soldering on a letter, etc., is made by adding 25 per cent bismuth to 50-50 solder (Fig. 5).

Procedure to Be Followed in Welding or Fusing

Scraps of pewter are used, *not solder;* they may be fused with a clean soldering bit or with a sharp pointed flame from a mouth blowpipe. No close fitting is necessary.

1. Wrap a piece of cloth smoothly around a stick of wood and fasten it in the bench vise in a horizontal position (Fig. 4).
2. Hang the work on the stick and swab the joint with the flux.
3. Place pieces of *pewter* along the joint.
4. Heat, clean, and tin the soldering bit, using pewter instead of solder for the tinning.
5. Apply the hot bit to the joint, moving it slowly so as to fuse the small pieces of pewter (Fig. 4).
6. Rinse the work in water, then file and scrape away the surplus metal.

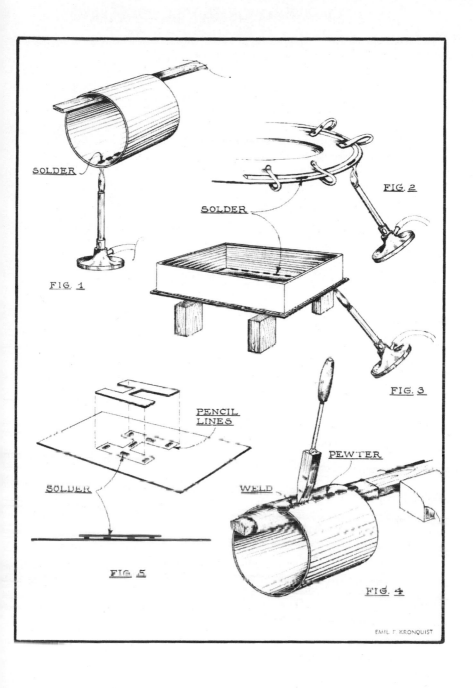

SOLDER

FIG. 1

FIG. 2

SOLDER

FIG. 3

PENCIL
LINES

SOLDER

FIG. 5

PEWTER

WELD

FIG. 4

EMIL F. KRONQUIST

HARD SOLDERING OR SILVER SOLDERING

Hard soldering is a trade name given to the process of soldering where a high degree of heat is required to do the job.

Joints that have been silver soldered are strong and tough if correctly made. Silver alloyed with copper and zinc in various proportions is the medium used. The solder may be *easy* or *hard flowing*, which means that one melts at a lower temperature than the other, and not that hard soldering is hard to do. The process demands careful attention to details, from the fitting of the joint to the application of the heat. Confidence in execution comes with practice, as in any art.

Silver solder is used in wire or sheet form, depending upon the work at hand. Borax in some kind of combination is generally used as a flux for hard soldering. The flux protects the surface from oxidation at the high temperature that is necessary. The borax, when fused, leaves a protective glaze on the metal that excludes the air, thus preventing oxidation. A gas torch is used in applying the heat.

Procedure to Be Followed in Silver Soldering (Typical Example)

1. Check the joint. See to it that there is contact everywhere and that all wires or clamps are in place.
2. Cut slits lengthwise in the silver solder (Fig. 1).
3. Cut across to obtain pieces of the desired size (Fig. 2). Place them on the edge of the borax slate (Fig. 3).
4. Pour a few drops of water in the hollow part of the slate, dip the borax in the water, and grind in a rotary direction until a milky solution is produced. (This borax now suspended in water is called "flux.")
5. With a small brush, apply the flux to the joint.
6. Evaporate the water from the borax by holding the work over a clean blue flame (Fig. 4). When the water has evaporated, a thin white coating of borax is deposited on the work.
7. Pick up the solder with the tweezers, dip each piece in the borax, and place them on the joint to be soldered.
8. Place the work in the annealing pan. Boost it all around with coke. Be sure it lies level.
9. Heat the entire job rather gently at first, then concentrate the flame along the joint until the solder "runs" (Fig. 5).
10. Let the work lose its red heat. Cool in water, then remove all iron wires.
11. Place the work in the pickling solution for 5 or 10 minutes to dissolve the oxides and the fused borax.

The professional way to silver solder is shown in Fig. 6. Hold the torch with one hand and apply the solder (wire form) with the other. This requires much practice and close coordination.

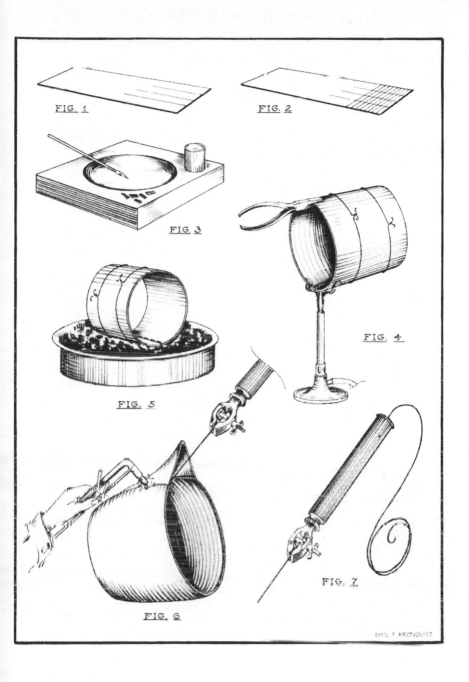

FIG. 1

FIG. 2

FIG. 3

FIG. 4

FIG. 5

FIG. 6

FIG. 7

EMIL F KRONQUIST

PATTERNMAKING

Often it becomes necessary to make a pattern so that an ornament may be cast. A pattern can be made in many different ways and in many different materials. It may be solid or split, and cored for hollow castings. Inasmuch as a mold of some kind has to be made either in plaster of Paris, sand, or metal, it is essential that the pattern be made with great care, because *a casting cannot be any better than the pattern from which it is made.* It must be smooth and clean and free from undercuts.

It is much easier to make a mold from a split wood pattern than from a solid one, and there is little difference in the time it takes to make it.

Material

Any dried, close-grained wood—white pine, cherry, or mahogany.

Procedure to Be Followed in Making (Typical Example, Fig. 1)

1. Glue two pieces of wood together, but insert a sheet of newspaper between the two glued surfaces. The combined thickness should equal the thickness of the pattern (Fig. 2).
2. Transfer the design to the wood (Fig. 3).
3. Place two small nails (brads) within the boundary of the design, as shown; hammer them into the wood just far enough so that the points are halfway through.
4. Saw out the design (Fig. 4).
5. File and finish with sandpaper (Fig. 5).
6. Apply two coats of orange shellac; sandpaper between coats.
7. Split the pattern by inserting the edge of a knife at the glued joint. The newspaper will split (Fig. 6).
8. Apply two thin coats of shellac on each half of the pattern.

The points of the brads have made tiny impressions so that the two halves will always check.

A spindle, as shown in Fig. 7, can be made in the same manner. A cup center must be used on the tailstock of the lathe, and wood dowel pins used instead of nails.

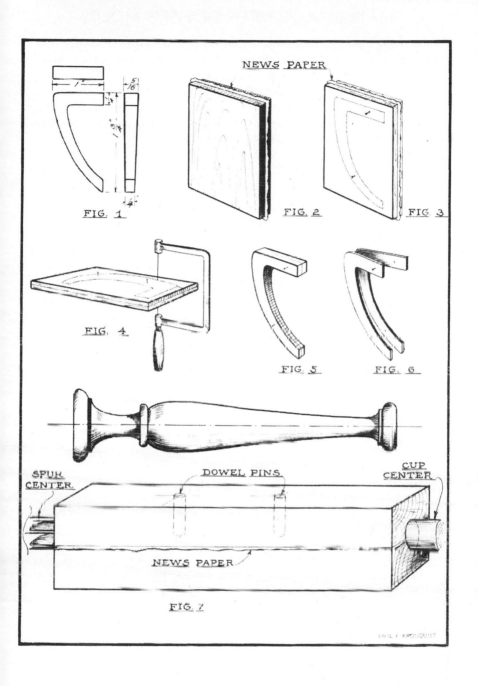

NEWS PAPER

FIG. 1   FIG. 2   FIG. 3

FIG. 4   FIG. 5   FIG. 6

SPUR CENTER   DOWEL PINS   CUP CENTER

NEWS PAPER

FIG. 7

EMIL F. KRONQUIST

MAKING A PLASTER OF PARIS MOLD

A mold made in plaster of Paris serves the purpose nicely for making castings in pewter, but it is not good for castings of metal that fuse at a high temperature.

A plaster mold, if carefully handled, can be used over and over again and stored for future use.

The pattern used for demonstration in making the mold is the split pattern that was explained on page 34.

Procedure to Be Followed in Making

1. Mount one half of the pattern on a smooth piece of wood.
2. Make a frame around the board (Fig. 1).
3. Grease the pattern and the entire inside of the frame. Use ordinary axle grease. Apply it thinly and evenly.
4. Pour some cold water in a container. Add plaster until it appears above the surface of the water, forming a state of saturation. Stir with the fingers until it feels smooth.
5. Pour the plaster into the frame. Give it a few sharp taps with a small hammer. This will detach any air bubbles from the pattern and make them float to the surface. The plaster of Paris will "set" or become hard in about 45 minutes.
6. Remove the frame, tap the board with a hammer, and pull apart. Figure 2 shows the first half of the plaster mold.
7. Cut or drill two shallow depressions for checks.
8. Make a wood frame around the plaster mold (Fig. 3).
9. Grease the mold and both halves of the pattern.
10. Press the whole of the pattern into the mold.
11. Fill the frame with plaster as before.
12. When the plaster has set, remove the frame and separate the molds with a thin knife blade, working from all sides gradually along the joint. Figure 4 shows the second half of the mold.
13. Cut the pour hole, or gate, and cut two air vents (Fig. 5).
14. Dust the mold with charcoal, pumice powder, or talcum.
15. Tie or clamp the two halves together (Fig. 6).
16. Melt the pewter in a ladle and pour it into the mold.

An interesting experiment may be found in making a plaster mold of a spoon or a fork. Use any piece of flat ware for a pattern. The pattern is placed on a board and blocked up with modeling clay to the edge of the pattern.

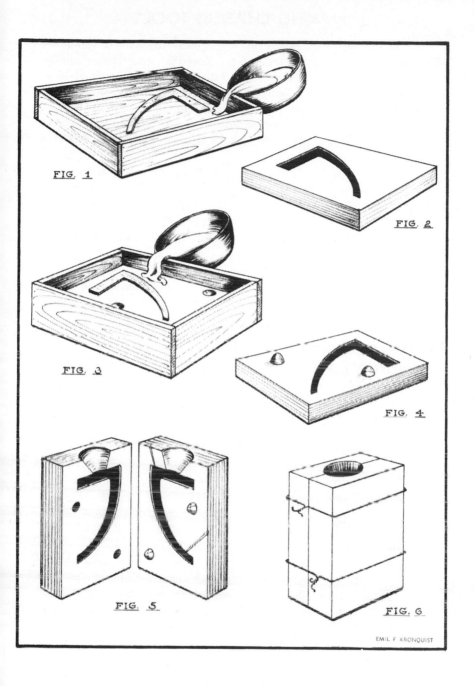

FIG. 1

FIG. 2

FIG. 3

FIG. 4

FIG. 5

FIG. 6

EMIL F. KRONQUIST

MAKING CHASING TOOLS

Chasing tools (Fig. 1) are made from various sizes of tool steel, filed or forged to rough shape (Figs. 2 and 3), and then carefully formed by fine filing to the shape demanded by the work at hand (Fig. 4). The finishing touch is put on the tool with emery cloth.

It is well to have stock on hand and make the tools as they are needed. Tool steel is purchased in 10-foot lengths. Sizes recommended are $\frac{1}{8}$, $\frac{3}{16}$, $\frac{1}{4}$, and $\frac{3}{8}$ inch square, all cut to $4\frac{1}{2}$-inch lengths.

After the tool has been made, it should be tried out and, if found satisfactory, hardened and tempered. Chasing tools are classified as:

TRACERS. All tools used for line work (Fig. 5).

PUNCHES AND PLANISHERS. All round- and flat-shaped tools (Fig. 6).

MATTING TOOLS. Tools having the ends dulled, or figured, by hammering them on a piece of emery cloth or an old file (Fig. 7).

BEADING OR HOLLOW TOOLS. Tools having various depressions (Fig. 8).

To Harden and Temper a Chasing Tool

1. Poke the point of the tool into a bar of soap and withdraw it. (The soap will release the black scale, oxide, from the steel in quenching.)
2. Grip the tool with a pair of pliers and heat the shaped point to a bright red color with a blow torch; then plunge it quickly into a glass of cold water (Fig. 9). The upper end of the tool should not be hardened.
3. Rub the end of the tool that has been hardened on a piece of emery cloth to make it bright. It is now ready for tempering. Keep the fingers off the bright part of the tool.
4. Light the Bunsen burner or an alcohol lamp.
5. Hold the tool with a pair of pliers and move it slowly through the flame. Avoid keeping the extreme point of the tool in the flame. By close watching a change of color of the steel will be noticed. When the point has taken a deep yellow hue, it should be quenched quickly in water (Fig. 10). This tempering process removes the brittleness caused by hardening.

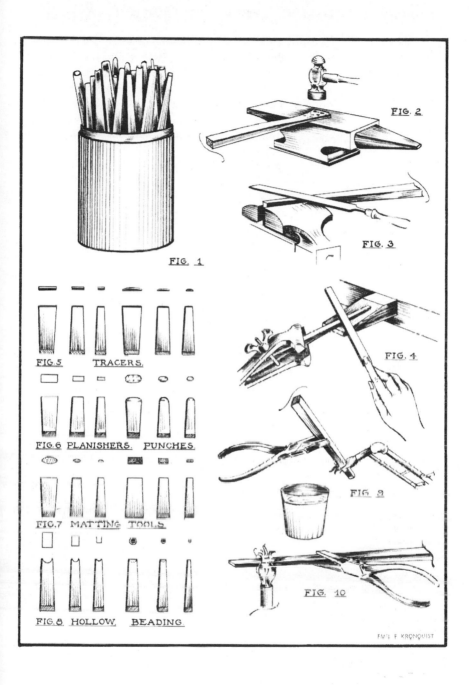

FIG. 1

FIG. 2

FIG. 3

FIG. 4

FIG. 9

FIG. 10

FIG. 5   TRACERS.

FIG. 6 PLANISHERS.   PUNCHES.

FIG. 7 MATTING TOOLS.

FIG. 8 HOLLOW.   BEADING.

EMIL F. KRONQUIST

PREPARING AND MIXING PITCH FOR CHASING

Pitch is the medium used as a supporting base in doing ornamental work on metal. It has no superior substitute and its preparation has changed little, if any, since the days of Benvenuto Cellini. Pitch cannot be used in its pure form but must have certain ingredients added to render it hard, but still resistant to the blow of the hammer without breaking or cracking. Pitch is indispensable in doing *repoussé* work. It should be prepared with great care. Once made, it will serve the craftworker for a long time. "Black shoemaker's pitch" can be purchased at a shoemaker's supply house for a few cents per pound.

Procedure to Be Followed in Mixing Pitch for Chasing

1. Place an iron kettle on a gas plate over a low fire. Put in 3 pounds of black shoemaker's pitch and 1 pound of rosin. Stir with a wooden stick (Fig. 1).
2. Add 6 pounds of plaster of Paris to the liquid mixture, sprinkling it in slowly by handfuls and stirring continuously.
3. Let the mixture simmer over a low fire for about six hours. Every trace of moisture must be evaporated. The chasing pitch is ready for use when it appears like a shiny, black, heavy sirup.

Chasing pitch can be tempered. If a harder pitch is wanted, add rosin; if a softer pitch is desired, add a very small amount of tallow or Venetian turpentine.

The illustrations show various ways of holding the pitch for working purposes.

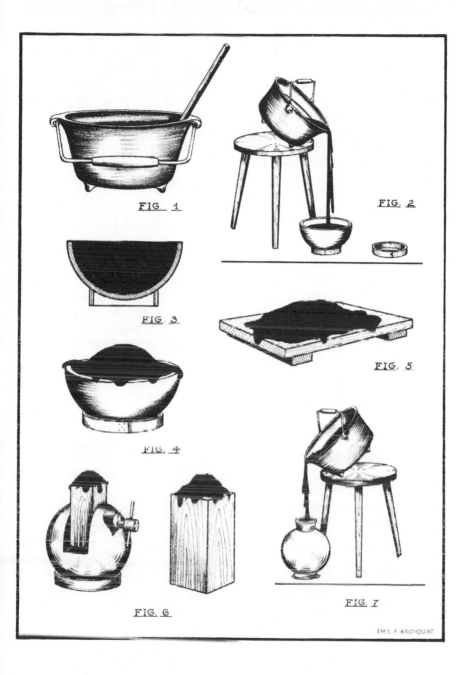

FIG. 1

FIG. 2

FIG. 3

FIG. 4

FIG. 5

FIG. 6

FIG. 7

EMIL F. KRONQUIST

ATTACHING THE WORK TO THE PITCH (CHASING)

Sheet metal, and sometimes the work itself, must be supported by some base material before any chasing can be performed. Pitch prepared in the proper manner furnishes the perfect base. Great care and patience must be exercised at times to build up the pitch while it is hot and in a plastic state. Scorched or burnt pitch loses its adhesive qualities.

The surface of the metal which is going to be in contact with the pitch should be oiled or greased a tiny bit. This will serve a twofold purpose: it makes the pitch stick better to the metal, and the metal can be removed from the pitch with greater ease when it is ready to be taken off.

Procedure to Be Followed in Doing a Typical Job

1. Begin heating the pitch, moving the flame slowly and at the same time revolving the bowl (Fig. 1).
2. Rest the flame and lift the bowl on to the supporting ring.
3. Push the warm pitch toward the center with a moistened thumb so that it forms a mound (Fig. 2). Let a moment or two elapse between heating and touching the pitch. If handled this way, a crust forms quickly and it will not stick to the fingers and cause a burn.
4. Repeat, if necessary.
5. Oil one side of the metal (the side that is to come in contact with the pitch) very sparingly with a drop of oil. Use the fingers or a small rag.
6. Reheat the pitch and, while holding the metal plate with a pair of pliers, place it on the top of the mound of pitch (Fig. 3).
7. Press it down into the pitch with a block of wood (Fig. 4).
8. When the pitch has cooled a little, build it up along the edges of the metal (Fig. 5).

Avoid air pockets under the metal.

Work may be cooled under running water (Fig. 6).

Hollow ware to be chased may be attached to the pitch (Fig. 7).

Small work may be attached to pitch piled on the end of a block of wood, as shown in Fig. 8. This, in turn, is to be held in an engraver ball.

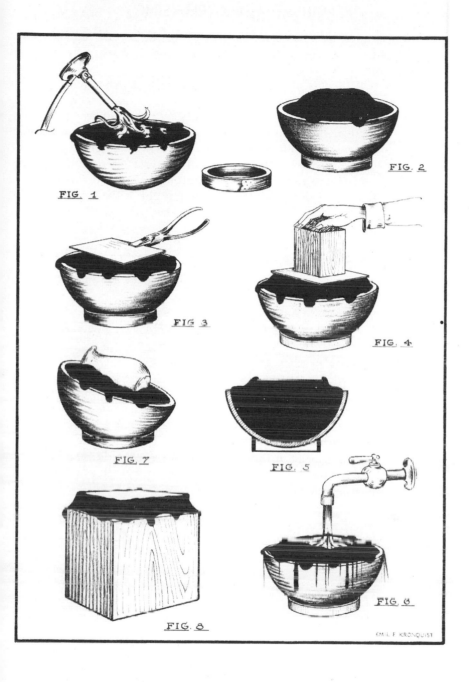

FIG. 1

FIG. 2

FIG. 3

FIG. 4

FIG. 7

FIG. 5

FIG. 8

FIG. 6

EMIL F. KRONQUIST

REPOUSSÉ WORK (CHASING)

An ornament hammered up in relief from the reverse side of a vessel or a piece of sheet metal is known as *repoussé* work (a French word meaning "to thrust back").

The actual process of tooling the metal with punches (chasing tools) and a small hammer is *chasing*.

The art of chasing can be mastered only by much diligent practice; an individual style and technique are acquired. *Repoussé* work may be justly called "sculpturing in metal." It was understood by artisans of all ages. Splendid specimens of the craft were found in Tutankhamen's tomb in Egypt. Down through the centuries, the art has found expression. Benvenuto Cellini, the artist, sculptor, craftsman, and writer of the sixteenth century, details the art of chasing in his famous autobiography.

Procedure to Be Followed in Making a Simple Practice Piece

1. Attach a piece of No. 20 gauge soft copper to the pitch (see page 42) and draw a flower or a leaf on the surface.
2. Select a tracing tool and outline the design (Fig. 1). Note, in Fig. 2, how the metal is stretched and not cut. The chasing tool should always be moved toward the worker.
3. Heat the metal with the Bunsen burner and remove it from the pitch with a pair of pliers (Fig. 3).
4. Wipe the metal clean with a rag and straighten, if necessary.
5. Attach the metal to the pitch, face down and, while the pitch is still slightly warm and plastic, the ornament is embossed or raised with round and oval punches. Remember that the work is being done in the reverse at this stage (Fig. 4).
6. Remove the metal from the pitch and clean it with a solvent, or still better, clean it by annealing.
7. Attach it to the pitch again and let it cool thoroughly.
8. The ornament is now modeled into the shape of the artist's conception with various-shaped chasing tools (Fig. 5).

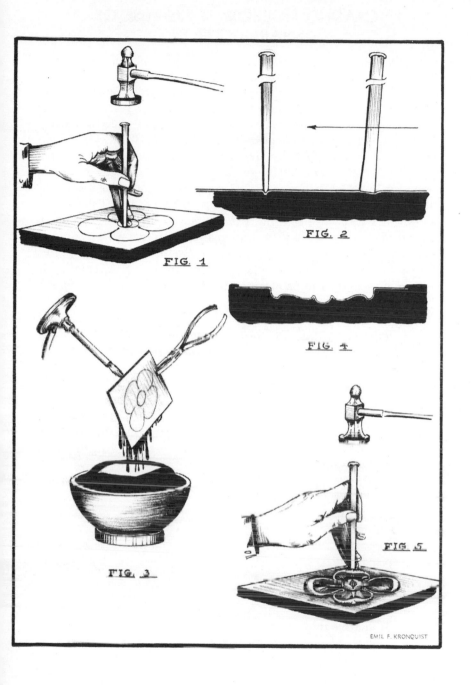

FIG. 1

FIG. 2

FIG. 4

FIG. 3

FIG. 5

EMIL F. KRONQUIST

CHASING HOLLOW WARE—USE OF SNARLING IRON

Obviously, it is impossible to use chasing tools and a hammer inside of a small vessel. Often hollow ware is decorated and ornamented with designs in relief. Such ornamentation must be done after the vessel has been completed.

An ingenious, simple, little tool of ancient origin, called a snarling iron, is used for raising, or pushing up, the necessary metal so that the design may be modeled in relief. The tool can be made from square steel, any size. The ends are bent to form right angles in opposite directions (Fig. 1). One end is left unfinished and the other end may be shaped to fit the work. Three different points are shown in Fig. 2. The snarling iron works by vibration and has a good deal of power. Fasten one end in a vise; strike it with a hammer and notice how it snarls. Time spent in practicing on old tin cans, the same way as is shown in Fig. 3, is time well spent. A remarkable degree of accuracy can be attained in raising an ornament or figure.

Procedure to Be Followed (Typical Example)

1. Transfer or draw the design on the work.
2. Use a fine steel awl and scratch the outline of the design on the metal.
3. Place the vessel on the snarling iron, holding it firmly with the left hand.
4. Tap the iron gently, as shown in Fig. 3. The purpose of this first little tap is to reveal to the operator the exact position of the point of the iron, which will be revealed in the form of a tiny bump.
5. Raise enough material so that the ornament may be modeled to the desired shape.
6. Oil the inside of the work very sparingly.
7. Fill it with pitch (Fig. 4) and let it cool.
8. Place the work on a pitch bowl, as shown on page 43, or place it on a sandbag. An old reliable way of holding the work is shown in Fig. 5.
9. Chase the outline of the design with a tracer.
10. Lower the background with a planisher.
11. Model the raised portion to the preconceived form.
12. Remove the pitch by melting it out with a flame (Fig. 6).

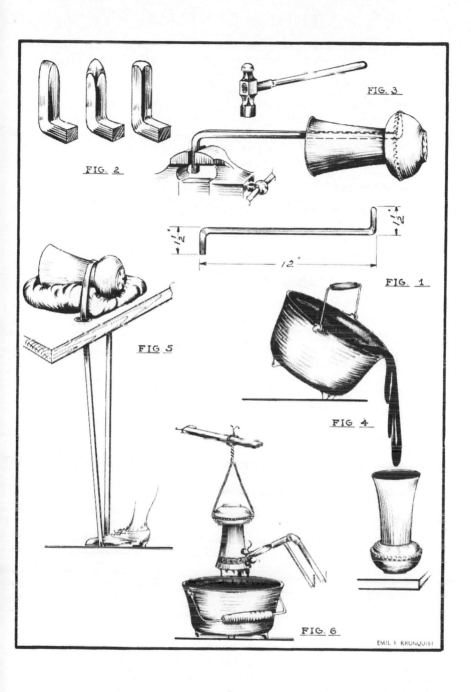

FIG. 2

FIG. 3

FIG. 1

FIG 5

FIG 4

FIG. 6

EMIL F KRONQUIST

1/2"

12"

1/2"

ETCHING OF METALS

The etching discussed here is entirely what may be called the "decorative" type, and is not to be confused with the art of etching or dry-point work which may be called "pictorial."

Decorative etching consists of painting the design on the metal with an acid-resisting medium, such as asphaltum, and then submerging the work into an acid solution that will eat all unprotected parts. The depth of the etching depends upon the length of time the work is left in the acid.

The success of a good job is attributed to meticulously prepared metal, good fresh paint, and a carefully painted design.

Etching Solution for Copper, Brass, and Pewter

To two parts of cold water, add one part of nitric acid.

Etching Solution for Aluminum

To two parts of cold water, add one part of hydrochloric acid.

Procedure to Be Followed

1. Clean the metal by scrubbing with fine pumice powder and water; rub in one direction only (Fig. 1).
2. Transfer the design to the metal (Fig. 2).
3. With a stylus, or a fine awl, scratch the design onto the metal, not too deeply (Fig. 3).
4. Scrub the metal vigorously with fine pumice powder and water to remove every trace of oil and grease. Rinse and dry. Do not touch the metal surface with the fingers; keep it covered with a clean piece of paper or rag and expose only the part that is worked upon (Fig. 4).
5. Paint the design with asphaltum, using a small water-color brush; also cover all parts of the work not to be touched by the acid. Dry overnight (Fig. 5).
6. Place the work in an enameled or glass tray. Pour in enough acid to cover the work. Rock the tray gently and use a feather to brush off bubbles that form on the work. It takes about 2 hours to etch copper, 1 hour for brass, and 10 minutes for pewter; that, however, is only the approximate time, depending upon the strength of the acid and the temperature.
7. Rinse in water, then remove asphaltum paint with turpentine or gasoline.

Aluminum has a coating of an invisible oxide that prevents the acid from biting into the metal at once. When the aluminum oxide has been cut, the acid will begin to boil violently and become hot and must be disposed of or poured into another vessel. After the first bite, fresh acid is poured over the work and the process is repeated until the desired depth of etching is reached.

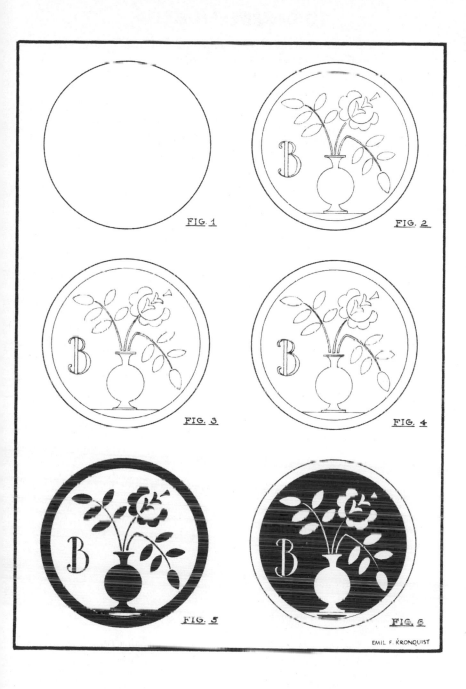

FIG. 1

FIG. 2

FIG. 3

FIG. 4

FIG. 5

FIG. 6

EMIL F. KRONQUIST

TO DESCRIBE AN ELLIPSE

1. Draw center lines at right angles to each other (Fig. 1).
2. Lay off the desired minor and major axes with a compass (Fig. 2).
3. Using half the major axis and the lower extremity of the minor axis as *center*, draw an arc cutting the major axis in two points. These are the two focal points (Fig. 3).
4. Place one pin at the extremity of the major axis and a second pin at the farther focal point (Fig. 4). Double a string or thread around the two pins; tie securely.
5. Remove the pin at the extremity of the major axis and place it at the other focal point, leaving the string around both pins (Fig. 5).
6. Insert a keen-pointed pencil in the loop and describe the ellipse (Fig. 6).

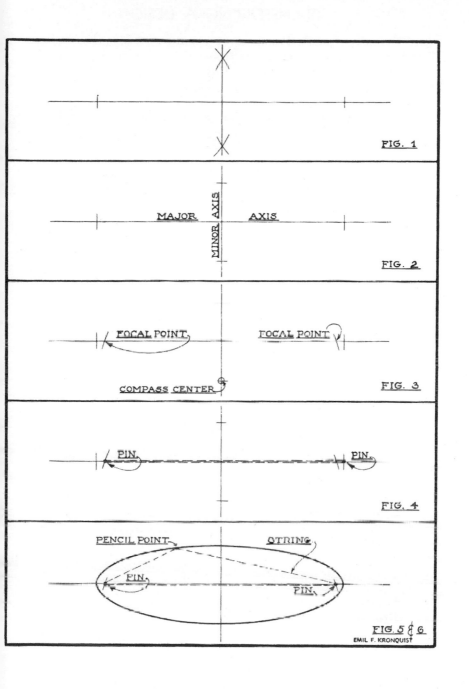

FIG. 1

FIG. 2

MINOR AXIS

MAJOR AXIS

FOCAL POINT

FOCAL POINT

COMPASS CENTER

FIG. 3

PIN.

PIN.

FIG. 4

PENCIL POINT

STRING

PIN.

PIN.

FIG. 5 & 6

EMIL F. KRONQUIST

TRANSFERRING A DESIGN

Beeswax is an ideal medium to use when a design is to be transferred from paper to metal, or from one piece of paper to another. In all cases, it must be used very sparingly. A piece of beeswax can be purchased in any drug or paint store.

Procedure in Transferring a Design from Paper to Metal

1. Scrub the metal clean with pumice powder and water; rub in a rotary manner.
2. Warm the metal over a Bunsen burner or alcohol lamp to about the temperature of boiling water. (Beeswax melts at about 145°F.)
3. Touch the heated metal with the beeswax, depositing a small amount.
4. Spread the beeswax over the surface of the metal with a small piece of a clean rag and let the metal cool and the wax harden. (An excessive amount of beeswax will defeat the purpose and result in failure to make a transfer.)
5. Place the design on the metal, face down to the waxed metal surface.
6. Rub a tiny bit of wax on the back of the paper to make it slippery.
7. With a burnisher, or the thumbnail, rub with firm hard pressure. The graphite, or black lead, from the pencil will stick to the beeswax and an exact copy of the design will have been transferred.

Transferring a Design from Paper to Paper with Beeswax

1. Prepare the paper which is to receive the design by rubbing it very gently with a small piece of beeswax.
2. Rub the back side of the design sparingly with beeswax. (The burnisher or fingernail will slide easily over the paper when this is done.)
3. Place the design where it is wanted, face down.
4. Rub it off with a firm pressure of the fingernail.

It is important to have a drawing with clean sharp lines. Printed matter may be transferred in the same manner.

PROJECTS WITH PROCESSES

COASTERS

Nothing is simpler to make than coasters of this type and a great many variations in the treatment of the edge can be made. Individual artistic skill may be displayed in working out different designs for etching. Animals, birds, flowers, and initials, ornamental or abstract, can be used.

The form used for turning the edge can be either wood or metal; however, metal is best. A piece of cold-rolled steel (shafting), 3 inches in diameter, about 4 inches long, should be used. Round the edge on one end and finish the surface with emery cloth, using No. 180 first, then No. 260. Finally, polish with crocus cloth. Apply oil to the cloth before using.

Material

Copper, soft cold-rolled, No. 18 gauge.
Pewter, No. 16.
Aluminum, No. 12.

Measurement

One $3\frac{1}{2}$-inch circular disk.

Procedure to Be Followed in Making

1. Clean the metal by scrubbing with pumice powder and water.
2. Planish carefully.
3. Draw a 3-inch circle with a compass on the back side of the metal disk.
4. Place the disk on the form and start hammering the edge down over the form a little at a time (Fig. 1). Use a mallet.
5. File and finish the edge with emery cloth.

Fluting and etching are optional.

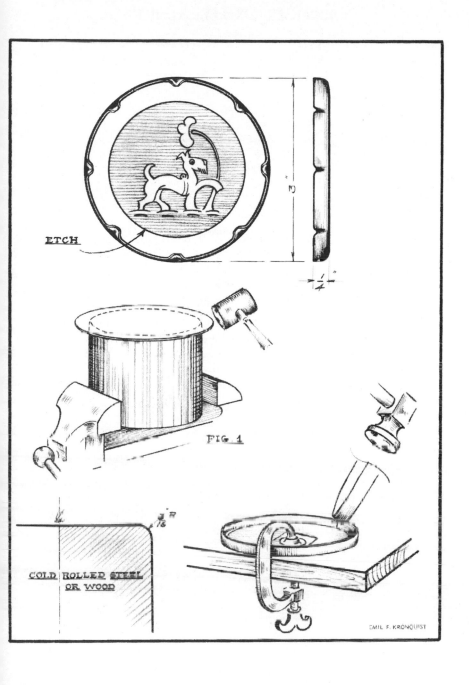

ETCH

3"

¼"

FIG. 1

R
1/16"

COLD ROLLED STEEL
OR WOOD

EMIL F. KRONQUIST

PORRINGER OR CEREAL BOWL

This design is a copy of a very old porringer, a museum piece. Today they are used for breakfast cereals and are very practical for servings for children. Monograms or initials could be worked into the design of the handle.

Material

Pewter.
Silver.

Measurements

Pewter: circular disk, 5½ inches in diameter, No. 14 gauge, Brown and Sharpe.
Silver: circular disk, 5½ inches in diameter, No. 18 gauge.
Handle: one piece, 2 by 2½ by ⅛ inch thick.
Fourteen inches of ⅛-inch half-round wire.

Procedure to Be Followed in Making (Pewter)

1. Raise the bowl with the ball-peen hammer. The successive shapes from each round of hammering are shown in Figs. 1 to 6.
2. Planish carefully with a highly polished hammer.
3. Flatten the bottom on a piece of steel that is highly polished (Fig. 7).
4. Level the bowl. Use a surface gauge for marking.
5. Fit and solder the half-round wire to the edge, as shown in Fig. 9.
6. File and finish the edge.
7. Transfer the design of the handle to the metal and scratch it with an awl.
8. Saw it with a jeweler's saw.
9. File and finish with emery cloth.
10. Fit the handle to the bowl and solder (Fig. 8).

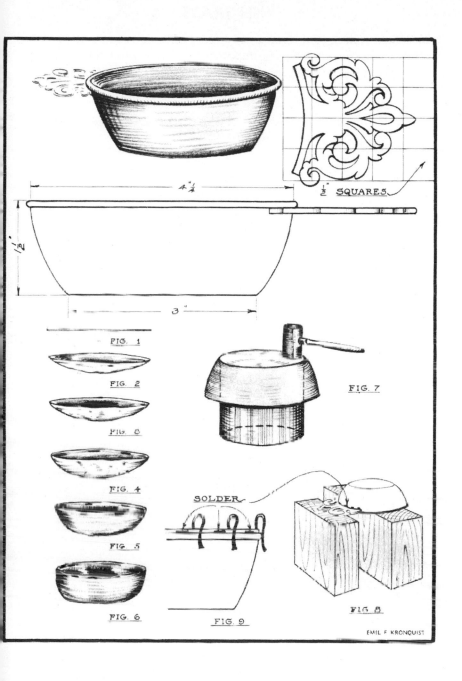

½" SQUARES

4 ¼"

½"

3"

FIG. 1

FIG. 2

FIG. 3

FIG. 4

FIG. 5

FIG. 6

FIG. 7

SOLDER

FIG. 8

FIG. 9

EMIL F. KRONQUIST

ASH TRAYS

When sinking a well on a tray, or a platter, or an ash tray—it is all the same—practice is important to do a good job. For the beginner, it is safest to use a block of hardwood, end grain, as shown in Fig. 1. When more experience has been gained in the control of the hammer, an iron should be used in place of the wood. The design of the rim should be cut after the center well has been sunk.

Material

Copper or brass.
Pewter.
Aluminum.

Measurement

One piece, 5 inches square, No. 20 gauge, Brown and Sharpe.

Procedure to Be Followed in Making (Copper and Brass)

1. Scrub with pumice powder and water. Select the better side of the metal for the front side.
2. Planish carefully with a highly polished planishing hammer.
3. Anneal and pickle the metal.
4. Straighten.
5. Describe a circle for the size of the well. Use a pair of dividers.
6. Prepare a hardwood block, as shown in either Fig. 1 or Fig. 2.
7. Start sinking the center (Fig. 2). Use a sinking hammer, as shown in Fig. 3.
8. Make the grooves (Fig. 4).
9. Cut the outside with a jeweler's saw.

Pewter cannot be annealed; it can be softened. (See *Annealing and Heating*, on page 6.)

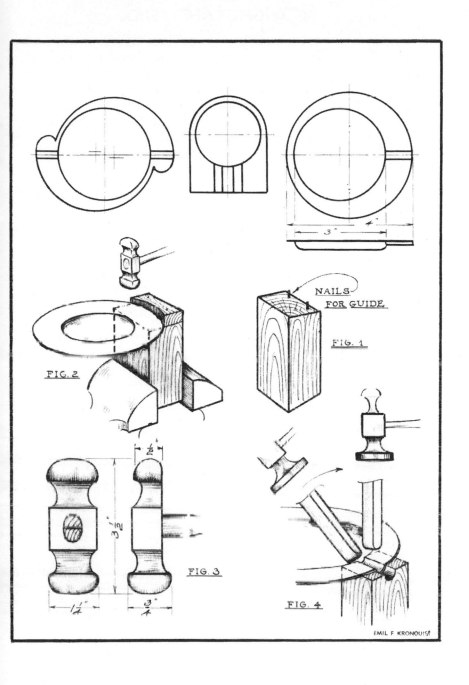

NAILS
FOR GUIDE

FIG. 1

FIG. 2

FIG. 3

FIG. 4

3"

4"

½

3½"

1¼"

¾"

EMIL F KRONQUIST

TWO-LIGHT CANDLESTICK

An attractive modern design may be made from standard stock sizes of metal parts. Copper, brass, bronze, and aluminum pipes can be purchased in innumerable sizes and wall thicknesses. Rods of many sizes are also stocked by dealers. A 1-inch slice of a 5-inch pipe with ⅛-inch wall forms the loop of this candlestick. The ring should be filed and finished before being cut; also, it should be scored at the place where it is bent.

Material

Copper or brass.

Measurements

One piece 5-inch o.d. tubing, ⅛-inch wall, 1 inch long.
Two pieces 1-inch o.d. tubing, $\frac{1}{16}$-inch wall, $1\frac{1}{4}$ inches long.
One slice of a 4-inch rod, $\frac{5}{16}$ inch thick.
One piece ⅝-inch round rod, ⅝ inch long.
Two pieces, 2 inches in diameter, No. 18 gauge.
One rivet, $\frac{3}{16}$ by $1\frac{1}{4}$ inches, round head.

Procedure to Be Followed in Making

1. File and finish the 5-inch loop.
2. Remove the waste by cutting with a hack saw.
3. Score the metal, then bend it.
4. Finish the base and sleeve.
5. Drill and countersink the necessary holes.
6. Hard-solder the 1-inch tubing to the circular disk.
7. Remove the center of the disk with the jeweler's saw.
8. Fit and soft-solder the candleholders to the main loop.
9. Finish all the separate parts.
10. Rivet the job together.

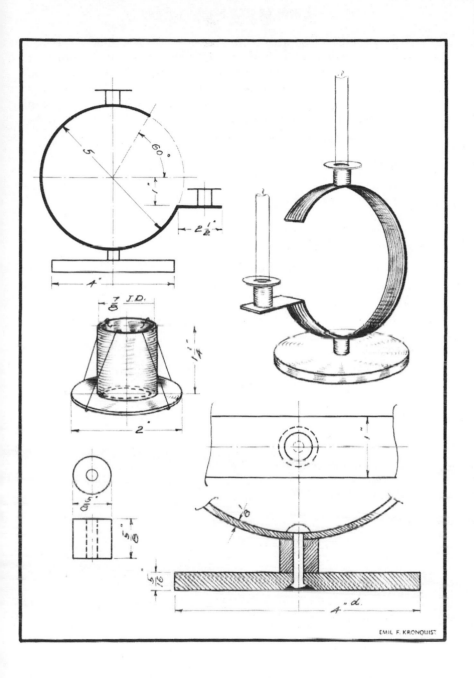

7 I.D.

60°

5

2½"

4"

1¼"

2"

5"

5"
8

5"
16

4" d.

8

EMIL F. KRONQUIST

6-INCH CANDY DISH

A small and shallow dish of this type can be made in many differ-ent ways. A common method employed by amateur craftworkers is the one shown in the illustrations and it is a perfectly good method, provided a good clean hardwood mold has been made for sinking the metal disk into (Fig. 1). In the absence of a mold, the metal can be hammered into shape with a ball-peen hammer, as shown on page 10 (*Shallow Hollowing*).

Material

    Pewter.
    Silver.
    Copper or brass.

Measurements (Pewter)

One circular disk, 6 inches in diameter, No. 16 gauge, Brown and Sharpe.
One strip, ⅜ by 7 inches, No. 16.
For silver, copper, and brass, use No. 18 gauge.

Procedure to Be Followed in Making

1. Prepare a mold (birch) with the contour of the dish (Fig. 1).
2. Planish the metal carefully.
3. Place it over the hollow in the wood mold.
4. Start hammering it into the mold; use a leather-covered mallet.
5. Make the lower ring.
6. Finish and trim the edge of the bowl to any desired design.
7. Fit the base to the bowl.
8. Solder the base to the bowl.

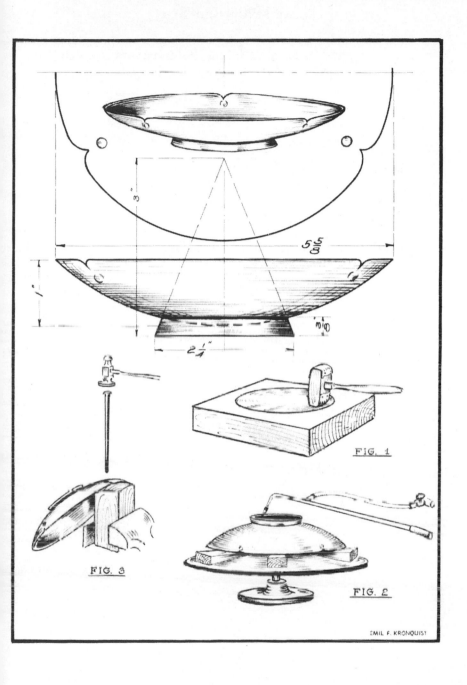

3"

5 5/8

1"

3/16

2 1/4"

FIG. 1

FIG. 3

FIG. 2

EMIL F. KRONQUIST

NAPKIN CLIPS

Odds and ends of metal may be converted into such things as napkin rings, clips, or buttons. Initials can be cut out of a different metal and soldered or riveted on, or they may be etched into the metal.

Material

Silver.
Copper or brass.
Aluminum.

Measurements

As shown in the illustrations; No. 18 gauge, Brown and Sharpe.

Procedure to Be Followed in Making (Fig. 1)

1. Planish a rectangular piece of metal to make it hard and springy.
2. Transfer the design to the metal and saw it out with a jeweler's saw (Fig. 4).
3. File and finish the edge of the metal with emery cloth.
4. Bend the metal, as shown in Fig. 5.
5. Saw out the initial.
6. Solder it onto the clip. (See page 28, *Soft Soldering*.)

Cold solder, a product that can be purchased in the hardware store, is satisfactory to use where an initial is to be attached to an aluminum surface.

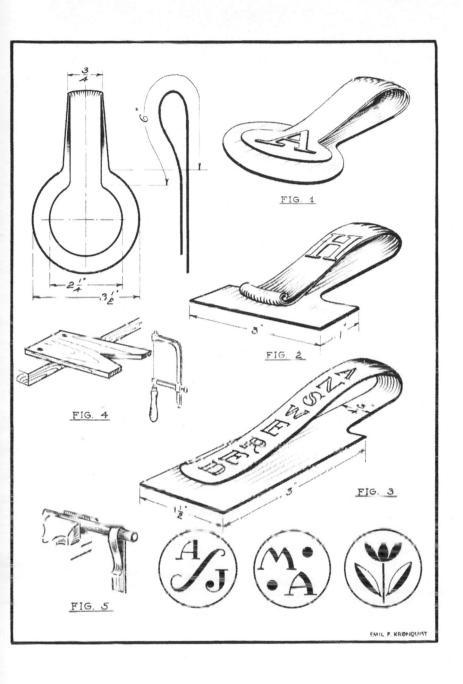

FIG. 1

FIG. 2

FIG. 4

FIG. 3

FIG. 5

EMIL F. KRONQUIST

STATIONERY HOLDER

A handy and useful gadget for any desk. This can have a very personal touch by the application of an initial, monogram, or insignia, such as the wings of the flying corps, on the front.

Combinations of metal are most attractive, as copper and brass (study Fig. 1), or aluminum with a brass base.

Material

Copper and brass combination.
Aluminum and brass combination.

Measurements

One piece, 6 by 7¾ inches, No. 18 gauge, Brown and Sharpe.
One piece, 2⅛ by 4⅝ inches, No. 20.
One piece, 2 by 4½ inches, No. 22.
One piece, ⅜ by 1¾ by 6½ inches.
Two rivets, ³⁄₁₆ by ½ inch, round head.
Four escutcheon pins. (Clip and use for rivets.)

Procedure to Be Followed in Making

1. Planish the 6 by 7¾-inch piece of metal.
2. True up the edges and round the corners with a file.
3. File and finish the base. Drill and countersink two holes for the rivets.
4. Make the decorative panel.
5. Drill all the holes for the rivets.
6. Rivet the decorative panels in place.
7. With an awl, mark the two lines where the metal is to be bent.
8. Bend to right angles.
9. Rivet the U-shaped metal to the base.

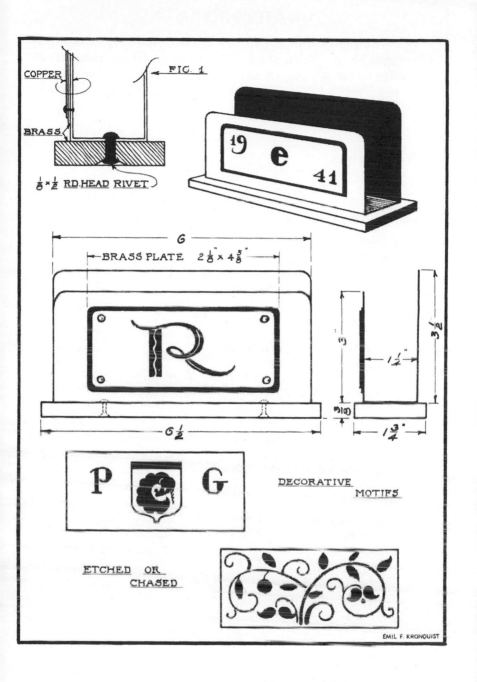

COPPER

FIG. 1

BRASS

$\frac{1}{8}'' \times \frac{1}{2}''$ RD. HEAD RIVET

19 e 41

G

BRASS PLATE $2\frac{1}{8}'' \times 4\frac{5}{8}''$

$6\frac{1}{2}$

3"

$1\frac{1}{4}''$

$3\frac{1}{2}''$

$\frac{3}{16}''$

$1\frac{3}{4}''$

P G

DECORATIVE MOTIFS

ETCHED OR CHASED

ÉMIL F. KRONQUIST

WATER PITCHER

The design of this pitcher resembles the shape so often seen in earthenware ewers. It is well adapted to being made in metal. The main body could be made from a single cylinder or hammered up from a flat disk; likewise, the handle could be made from two strips of metal.

Material

Copper or brass.
Silver.
Pewter.

Measurements (Made as Shown in the Illustrations)

Two circular disks, 7¾ inches in diameter, No. 16 gauge, Brown and Sharpe.
One piece, 3½ by 8½ inches, No. 16.
One strip, ¼ by 17¼ inches, No. 16.
One strip, ⅜ by 8 inches, No. 16.
One cast handle.

Procedure to Be Followed in Making

1. Make a full-size working drawing; enough dimensions are given to work out the details. The main body is spherical in shape.
2. Dome the semispheres (Figs. 1 and 2).
3. Planish carefully (Fig. 3).
4. Make the neck (Fig. 5).
5. Cut an opening in the upper half, a little smaller than the size of the neck.
6. Make the center band.
7. Make the ring for the base.
8. Fit all the parts carefully before any soldering is done.
9. Make a wood pattern for the handle, from which a casting should be made.
10. Fit the handle to the pitcher, then solder.

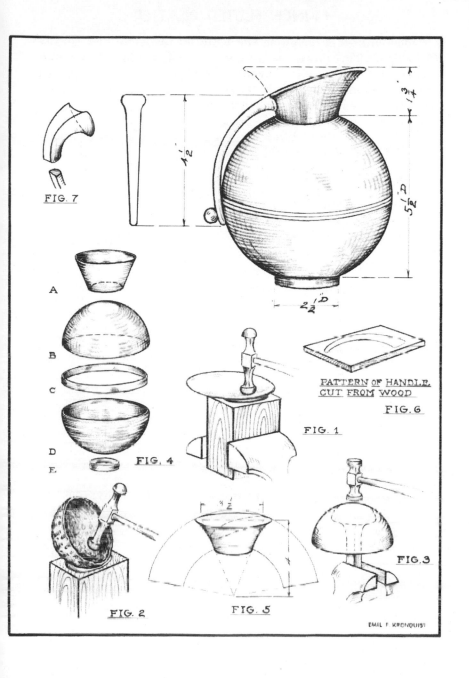

FIG. 7

A

B

C

D

E

FIG. 4

FIG. 1

PATTERN OF HANDLE,
CUT FROM WOOD

FIG. 6

FIG. 2

FIG. 5

FIG. 3

EMIL F. KRONQUIST

14-INCH FLUTED PLATTER

The process of hollowing the center of the metal disk is called "sinking." This process is used in the construction of trays and plates, such as the one shown in the illustration on the opposite page. The sinking line should be described with a divider, if a circle, and from a template, if any other shape.

Hardwood blocks are indispensable in doing metal work, as will be noticed from the pictures. It is used for sinking and straightening the plate; also, for doing the fluting on the rim, in this case.

Material

Copper or brass, soft cold-rolled.
Aluminum, soft.
Pewter.

Measurements

One circular disk, 14 inches in diameter, No. 18 gauge, Brown and Sharpe, for copper and brass; No. 14 gauge, for aluminum and pewter.

Procedure to Be Followed in Making

1. Scrub the metal with fine pumice powder and water; select the best side of the metal.
2. Scratch a circle, $9\frac{1}{2}$ inches in diameter, with a divider.
3. Prepare a hardwood block (birch); drive in two nails for stops.
4. Use an oval sinking hammer; strike lightly just inside the sinking line, rotating slowly (Fig. 1).
5. Straighten the plate (Fig. 2).
6. Repeat the sinking until the desired depth is reached.
7. Prepare a wood block for the fluting (Fig. 3).

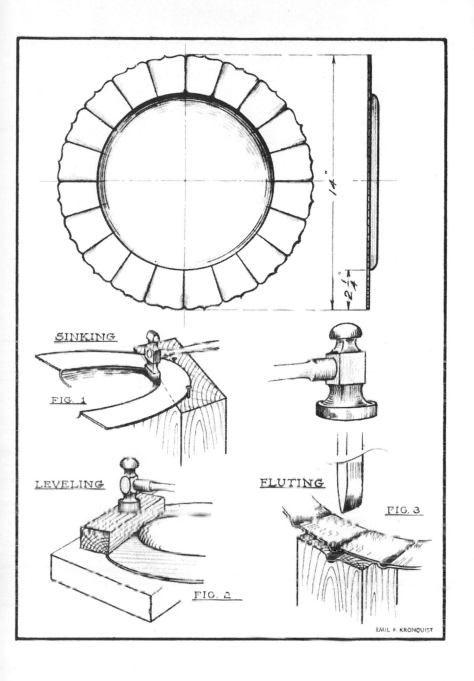

SINKING

FIG. 1

LEVELING

FIG. 2

FLUTING

FIG. 3

14"

2 1/4"

EMIL F. KRONQUIST

BEAKER

This beaker was sketched in a museum in Belgium. The original was made in silver, but it may well be made in pewter. It is modern in design and not difficult to make. The squared diagram shows the exact shape of the contour. When made in pewter, the seam should be fused or "welded" so that there will be no difference in the color of the metal (see page 30). The balls can be turned from solid stock.

Material

Silver.
Pewter.

Measurements (Silver)

One piece, 6 by 11 inches, No. 18 gauge, Brown and Sharpe.
Four pieces, $\frac{1}{4}$ by $\frac{3}{8}$ by $5\frac{1}{2}$ inches.
One circular disk, $3\frac{3}{4}$ inches in diameter, $\frac{1}{8}$ inch thick.
One circular disk, $3\frac{1}{4}$ inches in diameter, $\frac{3}{32}$ inch thick.
Four $\frac{3}{8}$-inch balls.

When pewter is used, the 6 by 11-inch piece should be No. 16 gauge metal.

Procedure to Be Followed in Making (Silver)

1. Make a full-size, detailed, working drawing.
2. Cut the segment of metal to form the truncated cone (Fig. 1).
3. Bend and tie together with iron wire (Fig. 5).
4. Solder the seam with hard-flowing silver solder.
5. Clean by pickling.
6. Even up the seam by filing, scraping, and hammering.
7. Shape it as shown in Figs. 2 and 3 and planish at the same time.
8. Solder the beaker to the base.
9. Solder the supports in place.
10. Solder the balls in place.

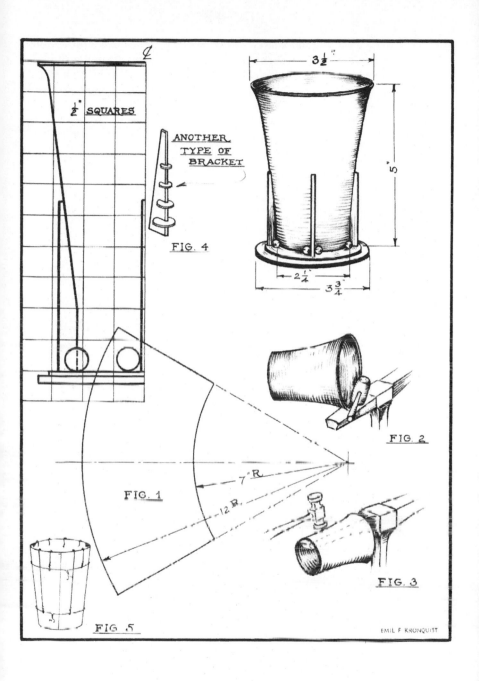

½" SQUARES

ANOTHER TYPE OF BRACKET

FIG. 4

3½"

5"

2¼"

3¾"

FIG. 2

7" R

FIG. 1

12 R.

FIG. 3

FIG. 5

EMIL F. KRONQUIST

PITCHER

The capacity of this vessel is 1 quart. The lines are simple and it takes but a few tools to make it. A full-size working drawing should always be made before the work is started. It gives the worker an opportunity to study the details of construction. Notice particularly, in Fig. 6, the way the bottom is placed.

Material

Copper or brass.
Silver.
Pewter.

Measurements (Copper, Brass, or Silver)

One piece, $5\frac{1}{2}$ by $15\frac{3}{4}$ inches, No. 18 gauge, Brown and Sharpe.
One piece, $3\frac{1}{2}$ by $9\frac{1}{2}$ inches, No. 18.
One piece, 2 by 3 inches, No. 18.
One circular disk, $3\frac{1}{2}$ inches, No. 18.
One piece, $\frac{3}{16}$ by $\frac{5}{8}$ by $7\frac{1}{2}$ inches long.

If the pitcher is made in pewter, the gauge of the metal should be No. 16.

Procedure to Be Followed in Making

1. Bend the metal to form a cylinder; tie it with iron binding wire, No. 16.
2. Solder with hard-flowing silver solder. Clean by pickling.
3. Start shaping the vessel (Fig. 2).
4. Planish carefully; use a highly polished hammer (Fig. 3).
5. Make the neck (Fig. 4).
6. Make the spout (Fig. 5). Shape a piece of wood as shown.
7. Solder the neck to the main body.
8. Solder the spout to the neck.
9. Forge the stock for the handle to a gradual taper. File, bend, fit, and solder it to the pitcher.
10. Turn the edge of the circular bottom piece, fit it to the vessel, and solder (Fig. 6).

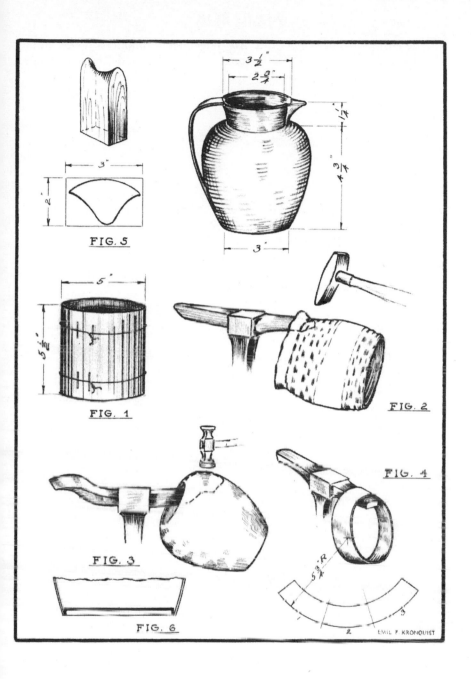

FIG. 5

FIG. 1

FIG. 2

FIG. 3

FIG. 4

FIG. 6

EMIL F. KRONQUIST

MAIL BOX

Accurate layout is essential. Any sheet-metal man can make the bends in a few minutes. The lettering should be made on separate pieces of metal and riveted on to the box. The spring is made from a $\frac{3}{32}$-inch round rod.

Material

Copper, hard rolled.
Brass, hard rolled.

Measurements

One piece, $10\frac{3}{8}$ by $15\frac{1}{4}$ inches, No. 22 gauge, Brown and Sharpe.
One piece, $4\frac{1}{8}$ by 6 inches, No. 22.
One piece, 3 by $5\frac{1}{2}$ inches, No. 22.
Three feet of $\frac{3}{32}$-inch round rod.

Procedure to Be Followed in Making

1. Select the poorest side of the metal and lay out all the lines shown in the drawings. Use a keen-pointed scratch awl and a try square.
2. Cut the pieces with a pair of shears; use a jeweler's saw where it is not possible to cut with the snips.
3. Bend to shape on a sheet-metalworker's "brake."
4. Solder the box together.
5. Fit and solder the bottom in place.
6. Make the hinges and do the fitting.
7. Make the name plate.
8. Rivet to the box.
9. Make the spring shown in Fig. 1.
10. Solder the spring to the bottom.

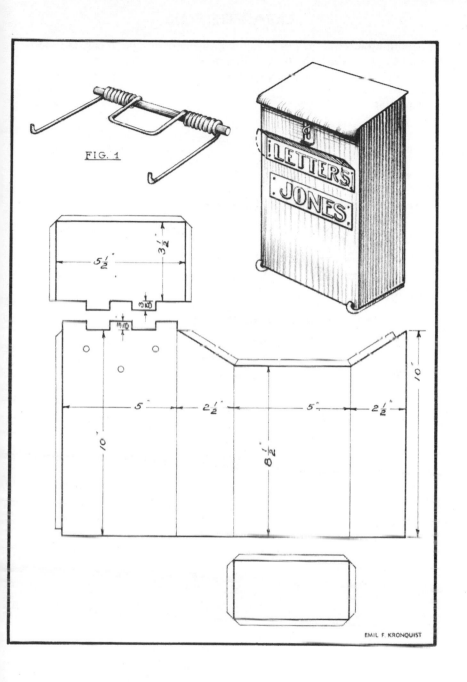

FIG. 1

$5\frac{1}{2}''$ $3\frac{1}{2}''$

$\frac{3}{16}''$

$\frac{1}{16}''$

5" $2\frac{1}{2}''$ 5" $2\frac{1}{2}''$

10"

10" $8\frac{1}{2}''$

EMIL F. KRONQUIST

CIGARETTE BOX

A unique combination of metal and wood, simple in construction and easy to make. The lifts shown in Fig. 1 are trinkets in a plastic material picked up in the dime store.

Material

Copper or brass, soft cold-rolled.
Aluminum, soft.
Pewter.
Silver.

Measurements (Pewter or Aluminum)

One piece, $5\frac{3}{8}$ by $5\frac{3}{8}$ inches, No. 16 gauge, Brown and Sharpe.
One piece, $3\frac{5}{8}$ by $5\frac{3}{8}$ inches, No. 16.
Two pieces of wood, maple, $\frac{3}{8}$ by $1\frac{1}{16}$ by 3 inches.

When made in copper, brass, or silver, the gauge of the metal should be No. 20.

Procedure to Be Followed in Making

1. Remove all blemishes and scratches from the metal by rubbing with pumice and water; rub in one direction only.
2. Drill holes in the metal the size of the escutcheon pins.
3. Bend the box part (Fig. 3).
4. Nail the wood in place (Fig. 4).
5. Make the four $\frac{1}{2}$ inch deep cuts in the lid with a jeweler's saw before bending (Fig. 2).
6. Make the lift, drill the holes necessary, and screw it on from the inside of the box.

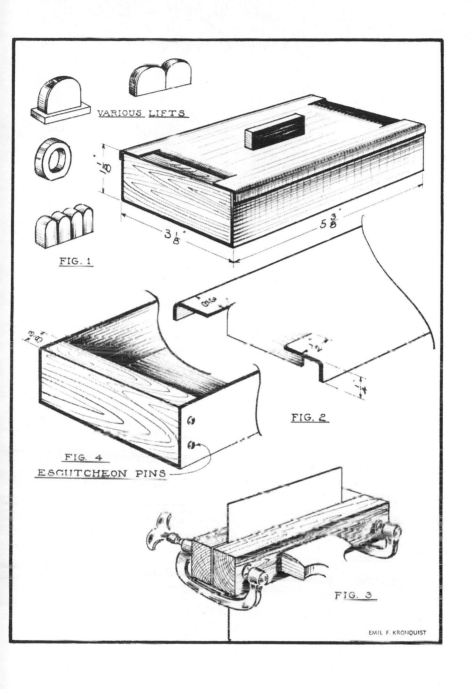

VARIOUS LIFTS

FIG. 1

$3\frac{1}{8}$"

$5\frac{3}{8}$"

$\frac{1}{8}$"

FIG. 2

FIG. 4

ESCUTCHEON PINS

FIG. 3

EMIL F. KRONQUIST

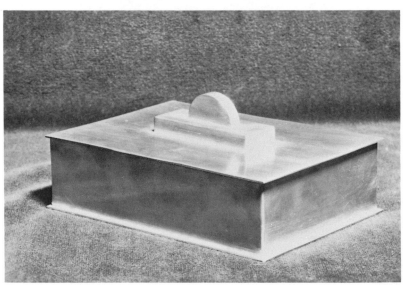

FLOWERPOT HOLDER

The holder as shown in the illustration, of course, must be made to the size of a flowerpot. The construction shown may be simplified by making the two main scrolls from rectangular stock $\frac{3}{16}$ by $\frac{3}{8}$ inches, then riveting or soldering the two together to form the center column, $\frac{3}{8}$ inch square.

A full-size diagram of the shape of the scroll should be made before the work is started.

Material

Copper or brass.
Aluminum.

Measurements

One piece, $\frac{3}{8}$ by $\frac{3}{8}$ by 26 inches.
(Alternate two pieces $\frac{3}{16}$ by $\frac{3}{8}$ by 26 inches.)
One piece, $\frac{1}{8}$ by $\frac{3}{8}$ by 36 inches.
Rivets $\frac{1}{8}$ by 1 inch, round head.

Procedure to Be Followed in Making

1. Lay out full-size drawing.
2. Split the square stock to the required depth (Fig. 1).
3. Remove the saw marks.
4. Bend the scrolls to conform with the drawing.
5. Make the loop the diameter of the flowerpot.
6. Drill the holes for the rivets.
7. Assemble.

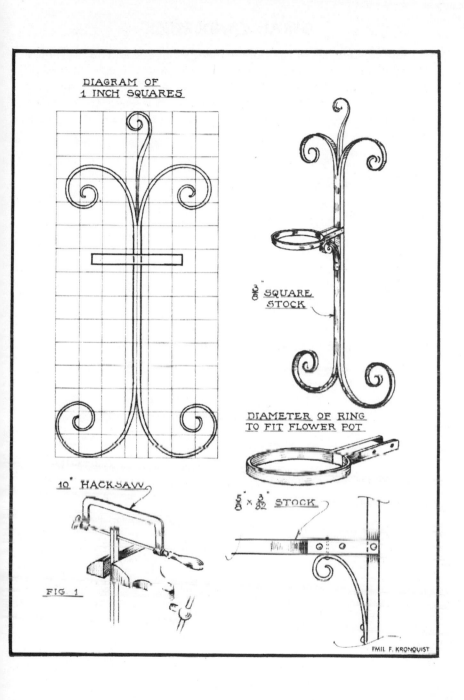

DIAGRAM OF
1 INCH SQUARES

$\frac{3}{16}$" SQUARE
STOCK

DIAMETER OF RING
TO FIT FLOWER POT

10" HACKSAW

$\frac{5}{8}$" $\times$ $\frac{3}{32}$" STOCK

FIG 1

EMIL F. KRONQUIST

SPIRAL CANDLESTICK

The twisted part of the candleholder should be laid out as shown in the diagram and filed and finished with fine emery cloth before it is twisted around a rod having a diameter of about ⅝ inch, as there is always a springback after twisting. It is suggested that the lower circular disk and the spiral be made of copper and the smaller disk be made of brass.

Material

Copper and brass.

Measurements

One piece of copper, 1½ by 9½ inches, No. 18 gauge, Brown and Sharpe.
One circular disk, 3½ inches in diameter, ⅛ inch thick, copper.
One circular disk, 2¾ inches in diameter, 3/32 inch thick.
One ⅞-inch washer, ¼ inch thick.
One rivet, ⅛ by ⅝ inch.

Procedure to Be Followed in Making

1. Saw the circular disks with a jeweler's saw, file, and finish the edges and surfaces.
2. Cut, file, and finish the spiral part.
3. Twist it around a dowel about ⅝ inch in diameter.
4. Drill an ⅛-inch hole through the three disks.
5. Countersink the holes.
6. Rivet the three disks together.
7. Solder the candleholder to the base.

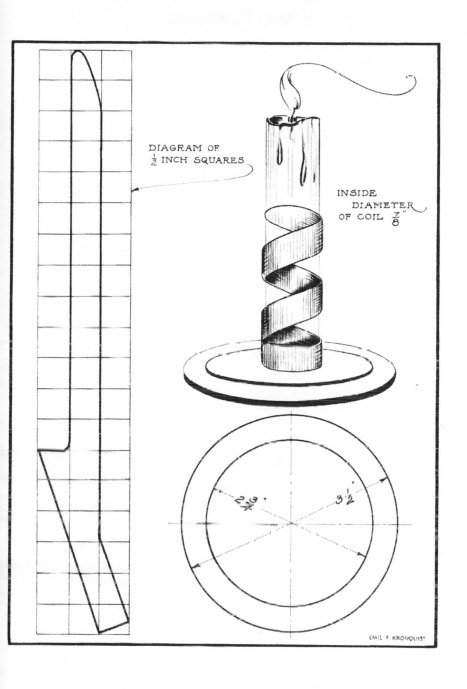

DIAGRAM OF
$\frac{1}{2}$ INCH SQUARES

INSIDE
DIAMETER
OF COIL $\frac{7}{8}$"

EMIL F KRONQUIST

WATER PITCHER

A practical and useful water pitcher with a capacity of 5 pints. It is not difficult to make. A wood pattern must be made of the handle, from which a metal casting should be made. When the pitcher is made of pewter, the handle can be cast in a plaster of Paris mold; however, the handle can also be forged from bar stock and filed to the final shape. A full-size working drawing with the developments should be made before the work is started.

Material

Copper or brass.
Silver.
Pewter.

Measurements

One piece, $7\frac{3}{4}$ by 20 inches, No. 16 gauge, Brown and Sharpe.
One piece, $2\frac{1}{2}$ by 4 inches, No. 16.
One circular disk, $4\frac{1}{2}$ inches in diameter, No. 18.
Handle, as shown in the $\frac{1}{2}$-inch squared diagram.

Procedure to Be Followed in Making (Copper, Brass, or Silver)

1. Cut the metal to the shape of the developed pattern (Fig. 1).
2. Prepare the metal for soldering as shown in Fig. 2. Use No. 16 annealed iron binding wire.
3. Solder with hard-flowing silver solder.
4. Remove iron wires, then pickle.
5. Start shaping the pitcher (Fig. 3).
6. Planish.
7. Shape the spout, fit it to the vessel, and solder.
8. Make the handle, fit it, and solder.
9. Solder the bottom in place.

When this job is made of pewter, the seam should be fused with pewter, as explained on page 30.

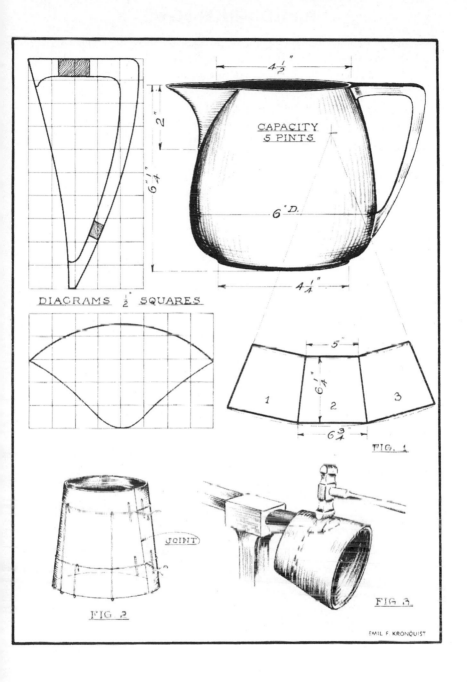

DIAGRAMS ½" SQUARES

CAPACITY 5 PINTS

4 ½"

2"

6 ¼"

6" D.

4 ¼"

5"

6 ¼"

6 ¾"

1   2   3

FIG. 1

JOINT

FIG. 2

FIG. 3

EMIL F KRONQUIST

FLUTED 9-INCH BOWL

Bowls of this size serve many purposes. They may be used for salads, flowers, or fruit and have decorative values when not in use. The fluting is done when the metal has been shaped and planished. As a rule, it is started in a grooved hardwood block with a raising hammer or a blunt chasing tool, as shown in Fig. 1. For finishing finer work, the bowl is filled with pitch and planished.

Material

Pewter.
Copper or brass.
Silver.

Measurements (Pewter)

One circular disk, 11 inches in diameter, No. 14 gauge, Brown and Sharpe.
One circular disk, $4\frac{1}{2}$ inches in diameter, No. 16.
One strip, $\frac{3}{8}$ by $8\frac{5}{8}$ inches, No. 16.
One strip, $\frac{3}{8}$ by 13 by $\frac{1}{8}$ inches.
When made in copper, brass, or silver, the circular disks should be No. 18 gauge.

Procedure to Be Followed in Making

1. Raise the bowl (see page 12).
2. Shape the base.
3. Make the intermediate ring (Fig. 2).
4. Planish the three units carefully with highly polished tools (Fig. 3).
5. Flute the bowl and the base (Fig. 1).
6. Make the lower base ring.
7. Saw out the center from the base shell.
8. Solder the lower ring to the base.
9. Solder the intermediate ring to the base.
10. Solder the base to the bowl.
11. File and finish the edge of the bowl.

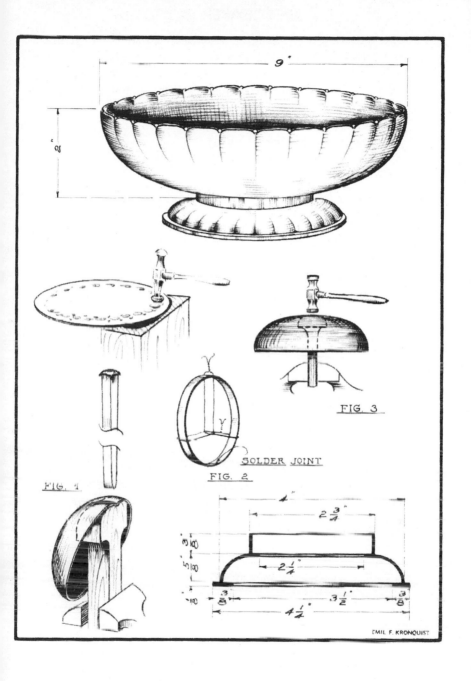

9"

2"

FIG. 3

SOLDER JOINT

FIG. 2

FIG. 1

4"

2 3/4 "

5/8"
5/100
1/8"

2 1/4 "

3/8"   3 1/2 "   3/8"

4 1/4 "

EMIL F. KRONQUIST

BEAKER

A table setting with drinking vessels of pewter or silver has a charm all its own. The individual touch may be given by the application of an initial soldered on to the beaker. If several beakers are wanted, a pattern should be made of the beaded ring (Fig. 5), and from this the necessary castings made.

Material

Pewter.
Silver.

Measurements (Pewter)

One piece, 5 by 9 inches, No. 16 gauge, Brown and Sharpe.
One piece, ⅜ by 4½ inches, No. 16, beaded ring.
One piece, ¼ by 10 inches, No. 14, lower ring.
One disk, 3½ inches in diameter, No. 16.

Procedure to Be Followed in Making

1. Cut stock, as shown in Fig. 1.
2. Curve, fit the joint, and solder.
3. Planish carefully (Fig. 2).
4. Stretch the lip by hammering.
5. Shrink the lower end with a mallet (Fig. 3).
6. Make the beaded ring (Fig. 5).
7. Make the lower ring for the base (Fig. 4).
8. Raise the 3½-inch disk and planish.
9. Fit the lower ring and solder to the base.
10. Cut a 2½-inch hole in the center of the base.
11. Fit and assemble the different parts.

The initial should be sawed out of No. 22 metal and soldered on with extra easy-flowing solder.

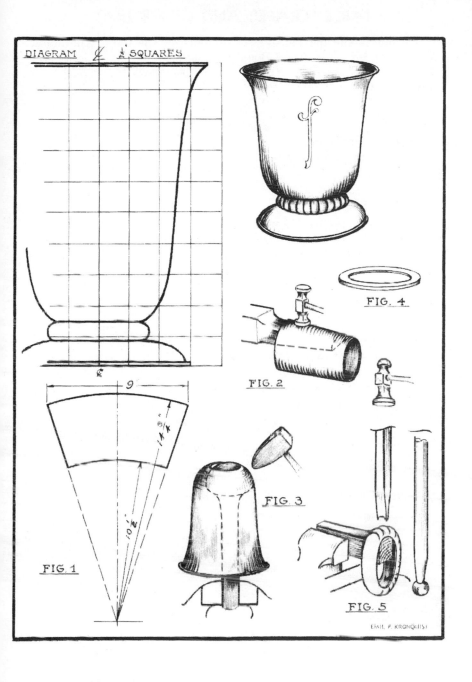

DIAGRAM ⊄ ½ SQUARES

FIG. 4

FIG. 2

FIG. 3

FIG. 1

FIG. 5

EMIL. F. KRONQUIST

TABLE SCRAPER AND CRUMB TRAY

A simple and inexpensive set of tools for the table. Aluminum trays with brass handles make a pleasing combination. Copper and brass go well together, also. A wood form must be prepared, as shown in Fig. 2.

Material

> Copper and brass.
> Aluminum and brass.
> Pewter.

Measurements

> One piece, $3\frac{3}{8}$ by $7\frac{3}{4}$ inches, No. 18 gauge, Brown and Sharpe.
> One piece, $\frac{1}{2}$-inch round rod, 4 inches long.
> One piece, $5\frac{3}{8}$ by $8\frac{3}{4}$ inches, No. 18.
> One piece, $\frac{1}{2}$-inch round rod, $4\frac{1}{2}$ inches long.

Procedure to Be Followed in Making

1. Prepare a piece of hardwood (birch) to shape the metal over.
2. Planish the metal carefully; strike harder along one edge to make it thin and knifelike.
3. Anneal and straighten the metal.
4. Shape it over the wood form.
5. File and finish the edges with emery cloth.
6. Cut a slot in the brass rod about $\frac{1}{4}$ inch deep. Use a hack saw.
7. Thin the edge of the tray by hammering to fit the groove in the rod.
8. Press in place.

An alternate handle is shown in Fig. 1.

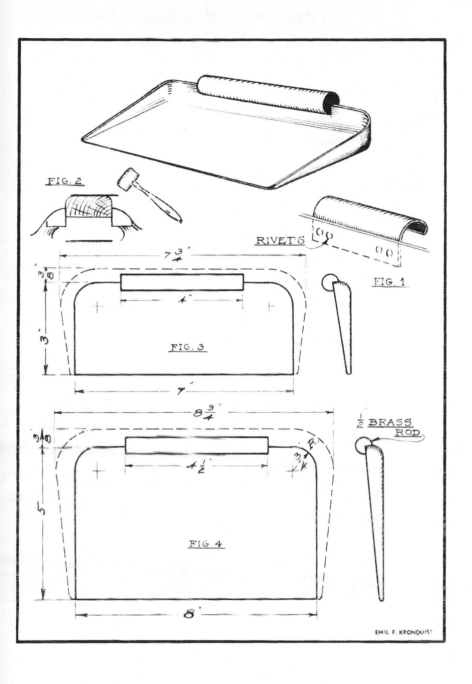

FIG. 2

RIVETS

FIG 1

$7\frac{3}{4}"$

$\frac{3}{8}"$

$4"$

3"

FIG. 3

7"

$8\frac{3}{4}"$

$\frac{3}{8}"$

$4\frac{1}{2}"$

$\frac{3}{8}"$R

R

5"

FIG 4

8"

$\frac{1}{2}$ BRASS ROD

EMIL F. KRONQUIST

CARD TABLE NUMBERS

This novelty can be made in several different ways. The numbers may be cut out of brass or bronze with a jeweler's saw and soldered to a copper or pewter base. Or they may be made of copper, brass, or pewter with the numbers etched into the metal.

Material

Copper or brass.
Pewter.

Measurements

Eight pieces, $1\frac{7}{8}$ by $2\frac{1}{2}$ inches, No. 16 gauge, Brown and Sharpe.
Thirty-two $\frac{1}{4}$-inch brass balls.

Procedure to Be Followed in Making (Pewter, etched)

1. Scrub the metal with pumice powder and water.
2. Draw or transfer the design to the metal.
3. Scratch the design with an awl.
4. Scrub again with kitchen cleanser.
5. Paint the design, number, border, and the entire back side of the metal with asphaltum (an acid-resisting paint). Let it dry overnight.
6. Prepare the etching solution. To two parts of cold water, add one part of nitric acid.
7. Immerse the metal in the etching solution, using a feather to brush off the gas bubbles that form on the surface.
8. Etch about ten minutes; rinse in cold water.
9. Remove the paint with turpentine or with any other solvent.
10. File a flat spot on the balls (Fig. 2).
11. Solder with 50-50 solder (Fig. 1).

The hammered edge is optional.

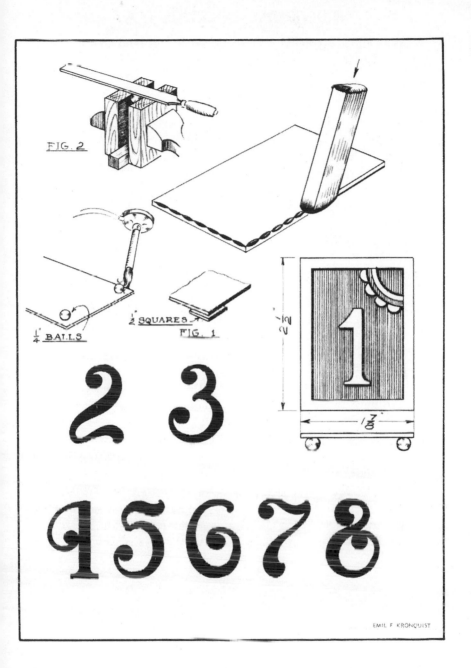

FIG. 2

1/4" BALLS   1/2" SQUARES

FIG. 1

2 3

4 5 6 7 8

EMIL F. KRONQUIST

INDIVIDUAL COCKTAIL TRAY

As an added attraction to a little tray of this kind an initial or an ornament may be etched or chased.

Material

Copper.
Brass.
Pewter.
Aluminum.

Measurements

For copper or brass, one piece, 5 by 7 inches, No. 18 gauge, Brown and Sharpe.
Aluminum, No. 12 gauge.
Pewter, No. 16 gauge.

Procedure to Be Followed in Making

1. Prepare a block of wood, birch or maple, $4\frac{1}{4}$ by $6\frac{1}{4}$ inches. Round the corners and the edges with a 6-inch wood rasp and finish with sandpaper (Fig. 1).
2. Clean the metal by scouring with fine pumice powder and water, or with kitchen cleanser.
3. Planish one side of the metal with a highly polished hammer.
4. Anneal the metal. (Pewter cannot be annealed.)
5. Straighten with a rawhide mallet.
6. Cut the corners round.
7. Place the metal on the wood form and begin hammering the edges of the metal over the form (Fig. 2).

Another way to do this is to make an extra piece of wood a little smaller than the form, then clamping the metal between the two pieces of wood, using the vise as a clamp for holding.

A suggestion for trimming or finishing the edge is shown in Fig. 3.

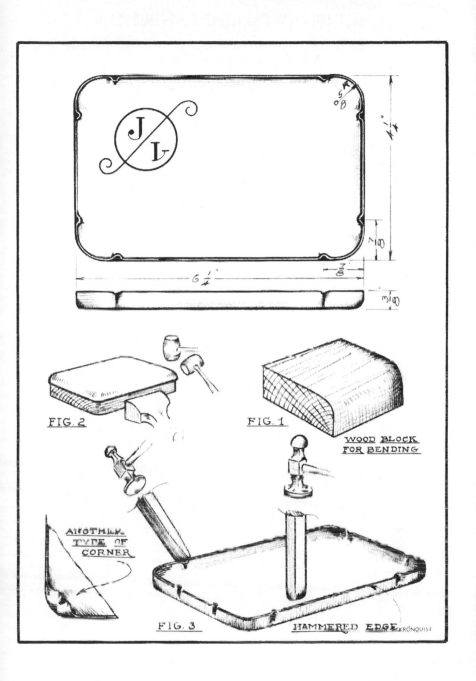

FIG. 2

FIG. 1

WOOD BLOCK
FOR BENDING

ANOTHER
TYPE OF
CORNER

FIG. 3

HAMMERED EDGE

MODERN TWO-LIGHT CANDLESTICK

This piece of fine design and excellent craftsmanship was sketched, with permission, at an art exhibit in Copenhagen, Denmark. It reflects in its lines what is generally known as "Danish silver," simplicity and strength. It might be improved by elevating the oval base slightly with four feet.

Material

Silver.
Pewter.
Copper or brass.

Measurements

One oval, 4 by 6½ by ⅛ inch thick.
One oval, 2 by 3¼ by 3⁄32 inch thick.
One strip, 1½ by 8½ by 3⁄32 inch thick.
One strip, 1¼ by 5¾ by 3⁄32 inch.
Two pieces, 2½ by 3¼ inches, No. 18 gauge, Brown and Sharpe.
Two disks, ¾ inch in diameter, ⅛ inch thick.
Two disks, 2 inches in diameter, No. 18 gauge.
Two pieces ¼-inch round wire, 2 inches long.
Two pieces ⅜-inch round rod, 2 inches long.

Procedure to Be Followed in Making

1. Lay out the two ovals (see page 50). Cut them with the jeweler's saw.
2. Form the two scrolls.
3. Lay out the cone-shaped candleholders; use a radius of 4½ inches, solder, and shape.
4. Solder the 2-inch disks to the holders.
5. File or forge the two stems.
6. Fit the different parts together.
7. Remove all scars and scratches with pumice powder and water.
8. Solder the component parts together.

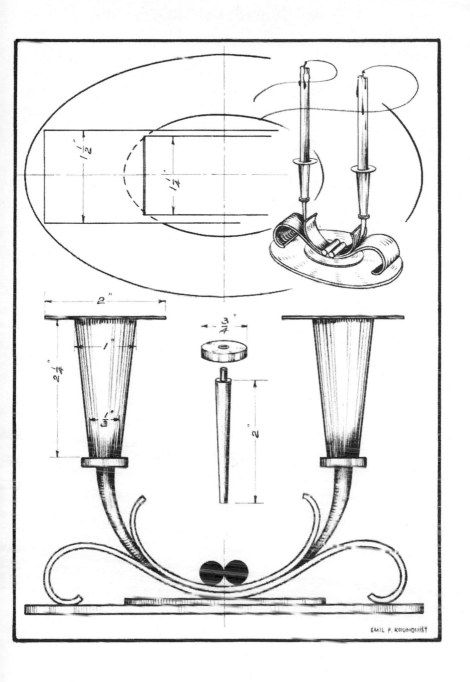

SIX SIMPLE ASH TRAYS

The ash trays shown on the opposite page are all simple in design and easy to make. Figures 1, 2, 5, and 6 are made like a plate with a sunken center. The outside shape can be cut with a jeweler's saw. The bowl on Figs. 3 and 4 is hollowed with a ball-peen hammer and the base may be stretched from a piece of tubing.

Material

Copper or brass.
Pewter.

Measurements

As shown in the illustrations.

The gauge of the metal should be No. 18 or 20, Brown and Sharpe, for copper or brass; No. 16, if made in pewter.

Procedure to Be Followed in Making (Figs. 1, 2, 5, and 6)

1. Scrub the metal clean, then planish carefully.
2. Anneal, pickle, and straighten. (Copper and brass only.)
3. Mark the center lightly; describe the circle with a pair of dividers.
4. Sink the center, using a plate or sinking hammer; straighten occasionally.
5. With a chasing tool and a hammer, and a block of hardwood as a support, make the groove (see page 58).
6. Mark the design; cut with a jeweler's saw.
7. Punch in whatever lines there are on the design.

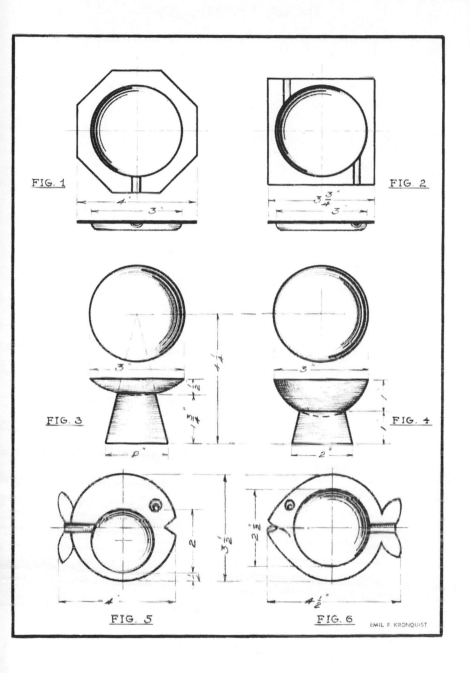

FIG. 1

FIG. 2

FIG. 3

FIG. 4

FIG. 5

FIG. 6

EMIL F. KRONQUIST

SMALL SERVING TRAY

A handsome little tray suitable for breakfast serving or for a sugar and creamer.

Material

Copper or brass, soft cold-rolled.
Pewter.
Silver.

Measurements

One circular disk, 10 inches in diameter, No. 18 gauge, Brown and Sharpe.

Two handle pieces, 2 by $3\frac{1}{2}$ inches, No. 14 gauge, Brown and Sharpe.

Two reinforcing wires below the handles, $\frac{3}{32}$ inch square, 3 inches long.

Procedure to Be Followed in Making

1. Planish the circular disk.
2. Anneal and straighten.
3. Prepare a forming block of hardwood, birch or maple (Fig. 1).
4. Describe a 9-inch circle on the back of the disk.
5. Place the disk on the wood form and hammer down the rim a little at a time with a rawhide or wood mallet (Fig. 2).
6. File and finish the edge of the tray.
7. With a chasing tool or punch give the edge a hammered finish (Fig. 4).
8. Saw out the handles with a jeweler's saw.
9. File and finish the edges, then fit them to the edge of the tray.
10. Bend and fit the square wire for reinforcement below the handle (Fig. 5).
11. Solder the handles and the square wire to the tray, using 50-50 wire solder (Fig. 3).
12. Clean and finish the tray.

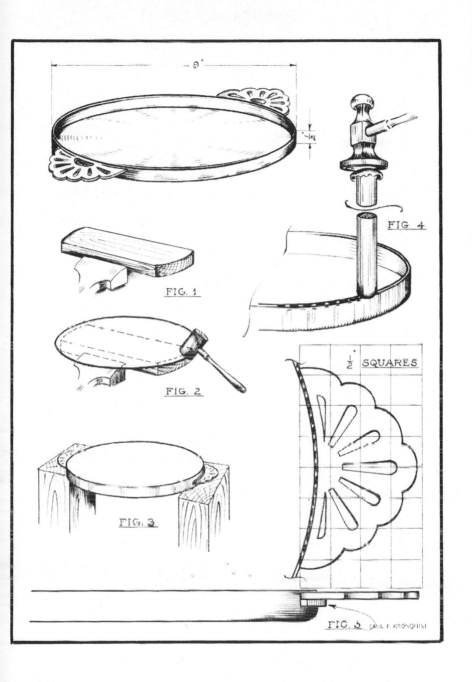

9"

½

FIG. 4

FIG. 1

FIG. 2

FIG. 3

½ SQUARES

FIG. 5   EMIL F. KRONQUIST

FLOWER HOLDER

A pretty little flower holder that can be made from short ends of metal tubing; almost any wall thickness will do. The oval base pieces should be laid out as ellipses (see page 50).

Material

Copper.
Brass.

Measurements

One piece of tubing, 2 inches o.d., $\frac{1}{16}$-inch wall, $4\frac{1}{2}$ inches long.
Two pieces, 1 inch o.d., $\frac{1}{16}$-inch wall, $2\frac{3}{4}$ inches long.
One piece, 2 inches i.d. by $2\frac{1}{4}$ inches o.d., $\frac{5}{16}$ inch long.
One piece, $3\frac{1}{2}$ by $5\frac{1}{4}$ by $\frac{3}{32}$ inch thick.
One piece, 3 by $4\frac{3}{4}$ by $\frac{1}{8}$ inch thick.

Procedure to Be Followed in Making

1. Lay out the ellipses on manila paper and cut them out. Transfer to the metal; use a scratch awl.
2. Cut the metal with a jeweler's saw, or drill a series of holes along the outer perimeter.
3. File and finish the edges with emery cloth.
4. Square the ends of the tubing. This can be done easily if a lathe is available.
5. Solder the narrow ring to the large pipe.
6. Rivet the two oval base pieces together.
7. Solder tubing to the base.

All scratches and blemishes must be removed from the metal before final soldering.

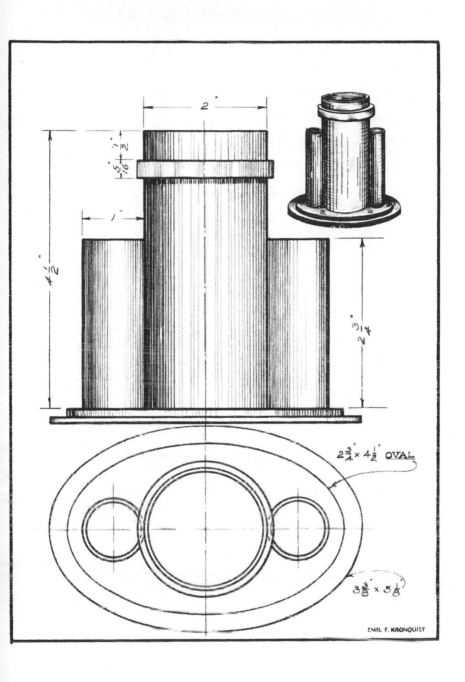

2"

5/16"   1/2"

1"

4 1/2"

2 3/4"

2 3/4" × 4 1/2" OVAL

3 3/8" × 5 5/8"

EMIL F. KRONQUIST

CRUMB TRAY AND CRUMB SCRAPER

Material

Copper, brass, pewter, or aluminum.

Measurements

Copper, soft cold-rolled, No. 18 gauge.
Brass, soft, No. 18 gauge.
Pewter, No. 16 gauge.
Aluminum, No. 14 gauge.

Procedure to Be Followed in Making

1. Planish the flat sheets of metal.
2. Anneal the metal to make it soft. This is not necessary if working in pewter.
3. Straighten the metal with a rawhide mallet on a clean flat iron.
4. Mark the part to be sunk like a tray with a scratch awl (Fig. 1).
5. Sink with a tray hammer to the required depth.
6. Straighten the metal again on the flat iron, using the rawhide mallet.
7. Mark the design and cut the outside shape with a pair of shears or a jeweler's saw.
8. Mark the two inside lines on the back of the job.
9. Raise the metal by using a punch or chasing tool, as shown in Fig. 2. This can be done on a piece of hardwood.
10. Mark the two inside lines on the back of the metal.
11. Raise the ridge by using a punch or chasing tool, as shown in Fig. 2. This can be done on a piece of hardwood.

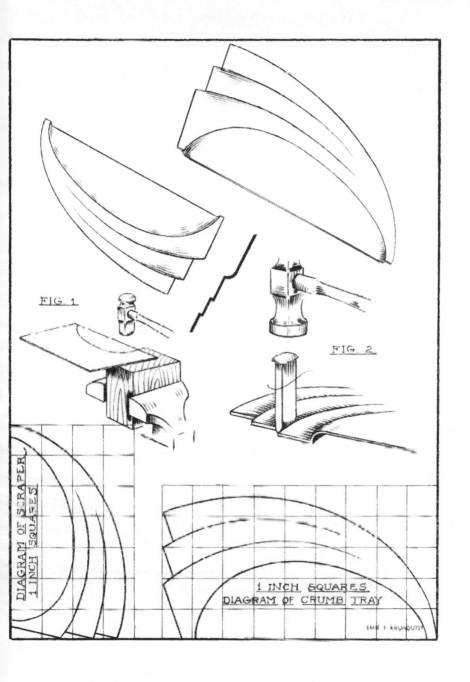

FIG. 1

FIG. 2

DIAGRAM OF SCRAPER
1 INCH SQUARES

1 INCH SQUARES
DIAGRAM OF CRUMB TRAY

EMIL F KRONQUIST

PLATTERS

The size of a tray determines the gauge of the metal from which it must be made; also the kind of material. The following schedule may be used for various sizes of platters, as shown in the illustrations on the opposite page.

FIG. 1

Material	Outside diameter, inches	Inside diameter, inches	Gauge
Copper and brass	10	6	18
Copper and brass	14	8	18
Copper and brass	16	9	16
Aluminum	10	6	16
Aluminum	14	8	14
Aluminum	16	9	12
Pewter	10	6	16
Pewter	14	8	14
Pewter	16	9	14

FIG. 2

Material	Outside diameter, inches	Inside diameter, inches	Gauge
Copper and brass	10	$6\frac{1}{2}$	18
Copper and brass	14	9	18
Copper and brass	16	10	16
Aluminum	10	$6\frac{1}{2}$	16
Aluminum	14	9	14
Aluminum	16	10	12
Pewter	10	$6\frac{1}{2}$	16
Pewter	14	9	14
Pewter	16	10	14

The copper should be soft cold-rolled to ensure a smooth surface. The aluminum must be ordered soft.
The sinking of the center of a tray is explained on page 70.

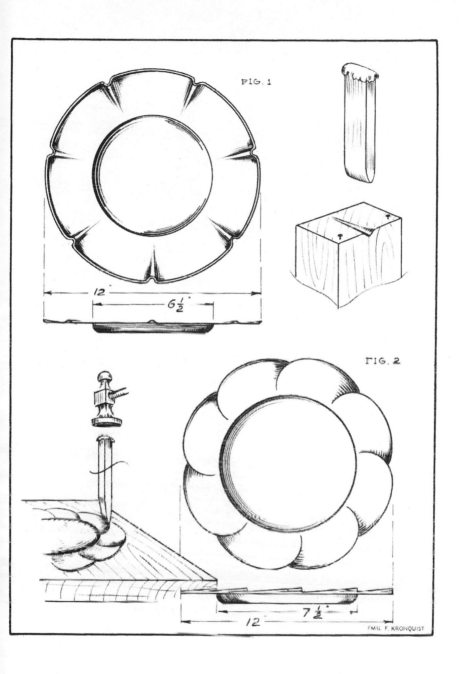

FIG. 1

12"

6½"

FIG. 2

12"

7½"

EMIL F. KRONQUIST

FLOWER OR FRUIT BOWL

A bowl of this size should be made of a heavy gauge metal, especially when made of a soft metal like pewter. Pewter is a very ductile metal and an 11-inch disk can easily be raised to a 3 inch height without softening the metal.

Material

Pewter.

Measurements

One circular disk, 11 inches in diameter, No. 14 gauge, Brown and Sharpe.
One 6-inch disk, No. 16 gauge.

Procedure to Be Followed in Making

1. Draw a few concentric circles on the disk for guide lines.
2. Place the metal on a sandbag and start hammering with a wood mallet having a rounded face; follow the guide lines until the center has been reached (Fig. 1).
3. Repeat the operation until the bowl is about $3\frac{1}{2}$ inches high (Fig. 2).
4. Describe a 3-inch circle on the outside.
5. Flatten the side on an iron stake (Fig. 3).
6. Flatten the bottom on a stake having a 3-inch diameter (Fig. 4).
7. Level by filing.
8. Raise the base in a similar manner as the bowl to about a 2-inch height.
9. Draw a guide line $\frac{1}{4}$ inch from the edge (Fig. 5).
10. Shrink the diameter to $5\frac{1}{2}$ inches (Fig. 6).
11. Remove a circular piece from the center by sawing; $2\frac{1}{2}$ inches in diameter.
12. Fit the base to the bowl.
13. Solder with 50-50 solder; place the solder on the inside.
14. Finish by rubbing hard with fine pumice powder and water; then rub with No. 0000 steel wool and soap water.

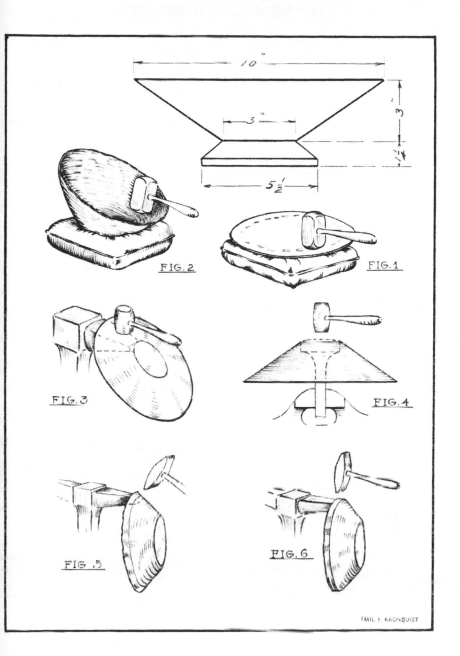

10"

3"

3"

½"

5½"

FIG. 2

FIG. 1

FIG. 3

FIG. 4

FIG. 5

FIG. 6

EMIL F. KRONQUIST

COMPOTE OR CANDY DISH

Shallow bowls, like the one shown in the illustration, when made in pewter, can be made in a wood mold. If a planished effect is desired, the metal should be planished before it is shaped in the mold. A mallet covered with a piece of leather must be used for hammering.

Material

Pewter.
Copper or brass.
Silver.

Measurements (Pewter)

One circular disk, 6 inches in diameter, No. 16 gauge, Brown and Sharpe.
One strip, $\frac{5}{16}$ by 7 inches long, No. 16.

Procedure to Be Followed in Making

1. Scrub the metal with fine pumice powder and water; rub in one direction only.
2. Place the disk in the mold and start hammering along the outer edge and work toward the center; do not hammer too hard. Little by little the metal will yield and take the shape of the mold.
3. Draw file the edge and finish the edge with fine emery cloth.
4. Bend the base strip to the curvature, as shown in Fig. 3.
5. Bend the curved strip to form a circle and solder with 50-50 solder (Fig. 4).
6. Fit the ring to the bowl and solder with extra easy-flowing soft solder.

When made in silver or copper, the gauge of the metal should be No. 18, and a ball-peen hammer should be used in the shaping. It should then be planished as explained on page 16 (*Planishing*).

The edge of the bowl may be enhanced as suggested in Figs. 1 and 2.

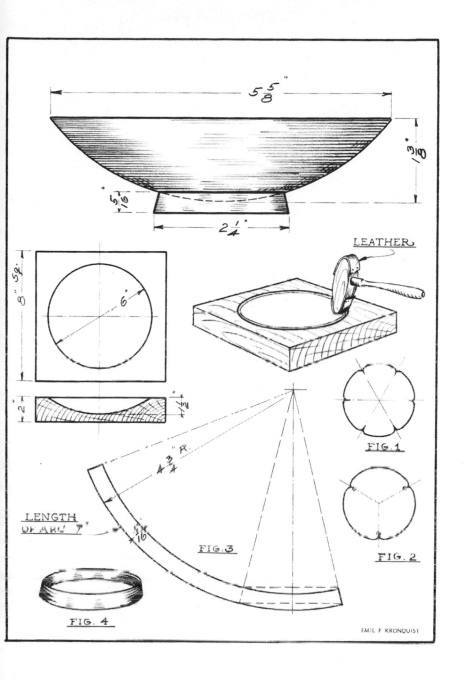

$5\frac{5}{8}"$

$3\frac{1}{16}"$

$\frac{5}{16}"$

$2\frac{1}{4}"$

LEATHER

$8\frac{5}{2}"$

$6"$

$2"$

$\frac{1}{2}"$

FIG. 1

$4\frac{3}{4}"$ R.

LENGTH
OF ARC $7"$

$\frac{3}{16}"$

FIG. 3

FIG. 2

FIG. 4

EMIL F KRONQUIST

CANDLEHOLDER

Material

Copper, brass, pewter, and aluminum.

Measurements

COPPER AND BRASS. The main disk is made from a 6-inch, No. 18 gauge, soft cold-rolled metal. The candleholder is 1 inch o.d., $\frac{7}{8}$ inch i.d.

PEWTER. The tray and the holder should be No. 16 gauge metal.

ALUMINUM. The 6-inch disk should be No. 12 gauge, soft, and the tubing 1 inch o.d. with a $\frac{1}{16}$-inch wall. Note in the sketch, in the lower left corner, how provision is made for riveting the candleholder to the base, as it is not possible as yet to solder aluminum.

Procedure to Be Followed in Making

1. Cut all the required stock.
2. Stretch the 1-inch tubing by hammering (Fig. 1).
3. Spread or flare the end of the metal for the handle; then planish and anneal (Fig. 2).
4. Hammer the 6-inch disk into shape, starting as shown in Fig. 3. Finish as shown in Fig. 4.
5. File the design on the end of the handle; then bend it to a right angle (Fig. 5).
6. Drill the necessary holes and rivet the handle in place.
7. Soft-solder the tubing to the base; place the solder on the inside of the tube.

Figure 7 shows how tubing can be made if the candlestick is made in aluminum.

The edge of the base may be made wavy, as shown in the sketch in the upper corner.

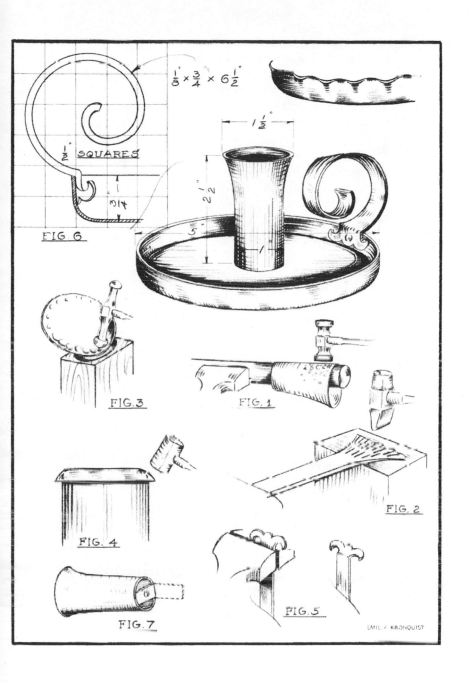

$\frac{1}{8}'' \times \frac{3}{4}'' \times 6\frac{1}{2}''$

$\frac{1}{2}$ SQUARES

FIG. 6

$1\frac{1}{2}''$

$2\frac{1}{2}''$

$5''$

$1''$

$3/4$

FIG. 3

FIG. 1

FIG. 2

FIG. 4

FIG. 5

FIG. 7

EMIL F. KRONQUIST

SERVING TRAY

A tray of this size is useful and can be trimmed to look very enticing, as one that was noticed in a garden restaurant in Sweden where it was used for *smörgås* servings. To make it more individual, a motif or a letter could be etched within a 6- or 7-inch circular field in the center. A piece of hardwood, birch or maple, 2 by 6 by 12 inches, must be prepared for the work, as shown in Fig. 4.

Material

Aluminum, soft.
Copper or brass, soft cold-rolled.

Measurements (Aluminum)

One disk, 18 inches in diameter, No. 12 gauge, Brown and Sharpe.
Ten pieces, $\frac{5}{8}$ by $3\frac{1}{4}$ inches, No. 12, made from corner cuttings.
15 feet of $\frac{3}{16}$-inch round soft wire.
20 rivets, round head, $\frac{1}{8}$ by $\frac{1}{2}$ inch.
If made in copper or brass, the gauge of the 18-inch disk should be No. 16.

Procedure to Be Followed in Making (Aluminum)

1. Scrub the metal clean with fine pumice powder and water.
2. Planish all the flat pieces carefully with a highly polished planishing hammer.
3. Anneal the planished pieces of metal. (See *Annealing Aluminum*, page 6.)
4. Straighten the metal (see page 20).
5. Draw with a pencil, on the back side of the metal disk, a guide line $\frac{3}{4}$ inch from the edge.
6. Fasten the prepared bending block in the vise and begin hammering the edge of the metal over the rounded edge of the wood (Fig. 4).
7. Twist three strands of the wire to form a rope (Figs. 1 and 2).
8. Form a ring the size of the tray and have the joint welded.
9. Form the brackets, drill the holes, and rivet the brackets to the tray.
10. Insert the rope in the loops and close them.

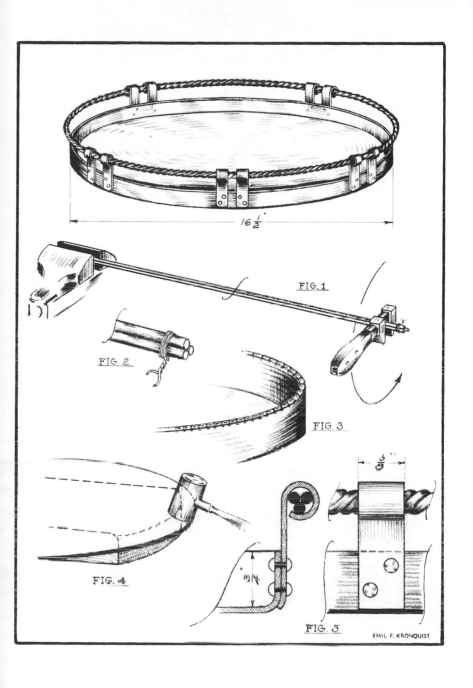

$16\frac{1}{2}$"

FIG. 1

FIG. 2

FIG. 3

FIG. 4

FIG. 5

EMIL F. KRONQUIST

LEAF TRAY

A great many varieties and forms of leaves are adaptable for trays and the sizes may be varied to serve any particular purpose, such as ash trays, card trays, or cocktail trays.

A rustic barklike appearance may be given to a piece of round wire by hammering, as shown in Fig. 2. The veining of the leaf should be done with a chasing tool (Fig. 1).

Material

Copper or brass.
Aluminum.
Pewter.

Measurements (Aluminum or Pewter)

One piece, 7 by 10 inches, No. 14 gauge, Brown and Sharpe.
One piece of round wire, $\frac{1}{4}$ by 7 inches.
Two rivets, round head, $\frac{1}{8}$ by $\frac{3}{8}$ inch.

If made in copper or brass, the gauge of the metal should be No. 18.

Procedure to Be Followed in Making

1. Cut or clip a pattern, as shown in the diagram. Use manila paper.
2. Mark the shape on the metal and cut it with a pair of shears and a jeweler's saw.
3. Clean the metal by scrubbing with fine pumice powder and water.
4. Planish the metal carefully.
5. Cut a forming block from a piece of 1-inch hardwood; size as shown by the broken line in the diagram.
6. Round one edge of the wood with a file.
7. Place the metal disk on the wood and hammer the edge of the metal over the rounded edge.
8. Finish the edge of the leaf by filing it smooth.
9. Wave the edge by gentle hammering.
10. With a blunt chisel and a chasing hammer (Fig. 1) vein the leaf.
11. Prepare and bend the $\frac{1}{4}$-inch round wire (Figs. 2 and 3).
12. Drill the holes and rivet the handle to the leaf.

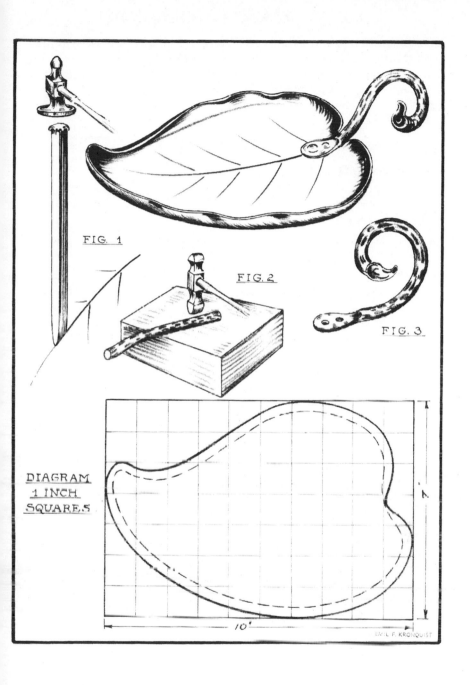

FIG. 1

FIG. 2

FIG. 3

DIAGRAM
1 INCH
SQUARES

10"

EMIL F. KRONQUIST

BUD VASE AND CANDLEHOLDER

This little combination was sketched in the Swedish pavilion at the Paris Exposition of Arts and Crafts. It is an idea good for further exploration with many possibilities. A glass test tube held by metal bands could be used as the flower holder.

Material

Copper or brass.

Measurements

As indicated in the drawing.

Procedure to Be Followed in Making

1. Hammer the $\frac{3}{16}$ by 1$\frac{1}{4}$-inch strip of metal so that it has a gradual thickness to $\frac{1}{16}$ inch.
2. Saw and file it to the size shown in Fig. 1.
3. Make paper templates of the two ovals; one 2$\frac{3}{4}$ by 4$\frac{1}{2}$ inches, the smaller one 2$\frac{3}{8}$ by 4$\frac{1}{2}$ inches.
4. Mark the ovals on the metal with a scratch awl.
5. Cut and file to sizes. (See *Cutting Heavy Metals*, page 4, Fig. 9.)
6. Cut the various pieces of tubing.
7. Square the ends.
8. Soft solder the $\frac{1}{4}$-inch rings to the ends of each piece of tubing.
9. Provide holes for screwing the two oval base pieces together.
10. Bend the scroll.
11. Fit the different members carefully.
12. Soft-solder the final assembly.

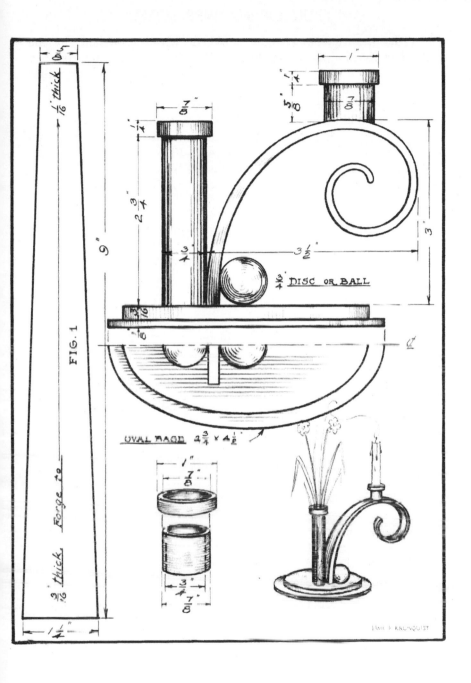

$\frac{1}{16}$" thick

$\frac{5}{16}$"⌀

FIG. 1

9"

$\frac{3}{16}$" thick Forge to

$1\frac{1}{4}$"

$\frac{7}{8}$"

$\frac{1}{4}$"

$2\frac{3}{4}$"

$\frac{3}{4}$"

1"

$\frac{5}{8}$"

$\frac{7}{8}$"

3"

$3\frac{1}{2}$"

$\frac{3}{4}$"⌀ DISC OR BALL

$\frac{3}{16}$"

$\frac{1}{8}$"

OVAL MADE $2\frac{3}{4}$" × $4\frac{1}{2}$"

1"

$\frac{7}{8}$"

$\frac{3}{4}$"

$\frac{7}{8}$"

EMIL F. KRONQUIST

FRUIT OR FLOWER BOWL

This beautiful bowl was sketched, with permission, in the Swedish pavilion at the Paris Exposition of Arts and Crafts. The original was executed in silver, but it may well be made in either brass or pewter.

To make the handles a pattern must be made, mahogany wood preferably, and castings made from this. Lay out a full-size drawing, as shown in the diagram. Saw, file, and carve the wood to the shape and sizes shown in the cross sections. Fine pewter castings are easily made in plaster of Paris molds. (See page 36, *Making Plaster Molds*.) Silver and brass castings must be made in sand molds.

Material

> Silver.
> Brass.
> Pewter.

Measurements

One circular disk, 12 inches in diameter, No. 18 gauge, Brown and Sharpe, for silver and brass; No. 14 for pewter.

One circular disk for base, 5 inches in diameter, No. 18 for silver and brass; No. 14 for pewter.

One strip, $\frac{3}{32}$ by $\frac{3}{8}$ by 13 inches, for base ring.

Two cast handles.

Two $\frac{1}{2}$-inch balls.

Procedure to Be Followed in Making

1. Hollow the bowl (Figs. 1 and 2).
2. Planish and level (Fig. 3).
3. Turn the edge of the bowl (Figs. 4 and 5).
4. Make the base (Fig. 6, *a*, *b*, *c*, and *d*).
5. Make the base ring (Fig. 7).
6. Solder the ring to the base.
7. Solder the base to the bowl.
8. Fit and solder the handles to the bowl.

The edges of the bowl may be enriched by filing it into units of scallops.

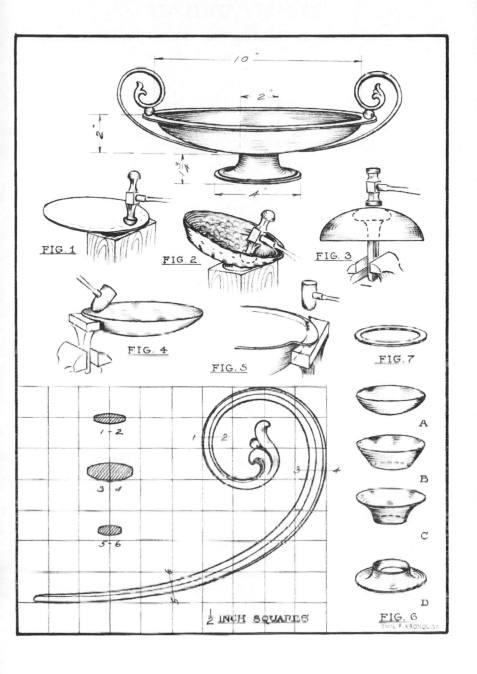

FIG. 1

FIG. 2

FIG. 3

FIG. 4

FIG. 5

FIG. 7

½ INCH SQUARES

FIG. 6

A

B

C

D

ERIC F. KRONQUIST

12-INCH CAKE PLATE

A simple little cake plate that can easily be made in pewter. The tool shown in Fig. 3 is called a jig and can be made in many sizes but should be carefully finished at the working end. It is a positive little tool to use and it works well. Do not bend all the metal at once; ease it along, bending it a little at a time.

Material

Pewter.
Copper (silver plated).

Measurements

One circular disk, 12 inches in diameter, No. 18 gauge, Brown and Sharpe.
One strip, ⅜ by 14 inches, No. 16.

Procedure to Be Followed in Making

1. Scrub the metal with fine pumice powder and water; rub in one direction only.
2. Planish the best side of the metal carefully.
3. Sink it, on a sandbag, with a clean leather-covered mallet (Fig. 1).
4. Smooth out the bumps (Fig. 2).
5. Turn the edge with the jig (Fig. 3).
6. Finish the job with a mallet (Fig. 5).
7. Make the ring and solder it on to the plate.

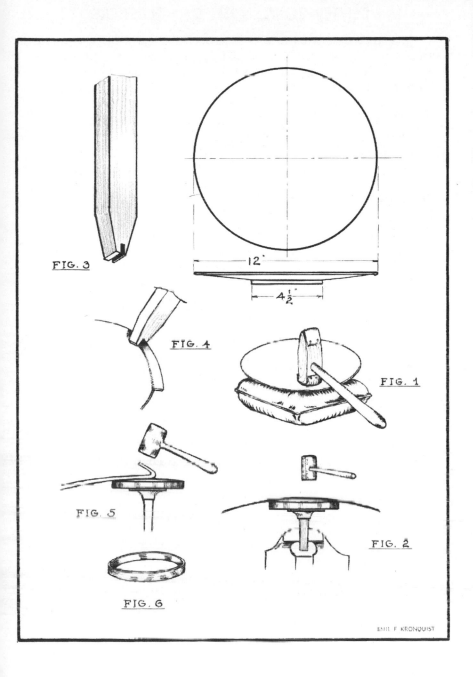

FIG. 3

12"

4½"

FIG. 4

FIG. 1

FIG. 5

FIG. 2

FIG. 6

EMIL F KRONQUIST

CENTER BOWL WITH CANDLESTICKS

A dignified set with a modern touch in design for use on the dining table or the side buffet. A tall candle held in a heavy clear glass holder can be submerged in the water and the flower arrangements made around it.

Material

Pewter.
Copper or brass.
Silver.

Measurements (Bowl—Pewter)

One circular disk, 11 inches in diameter, No. 14 gauge, Brown and Sharpe.
One disk, $4\frac{1}{2}$ inches in diameter, No. 14.
One strip, $\frac{3}{8}$ by 9 inches, No. 14.
One strip, $\frac{3}{8}$ by 13 inches, No. 10.
When made in copper, brass, or silver, the circular disks should be No. 18 gauge metal.

Measurements (Candlesticks—Pewter)

One circular disk, $4\frac{1}{4}$ inches in diameter, No. 14.
One circular disk, 2 inches in diameter, No. 14.
One piece, $1\frac{1}{4}$ by $3\frac{1}{8}$ inches, No. 16.
One strip, $\frac{5}{16}$ by $3\frac{1}{4}$ inches, No. 18.
One strip, $\frac{3}{8}$ by 12 inches, No. 10. Base ring.

Procedure to Be Followed in Making the Bowl (Pewter)

1. Raise the bowl with the ball-peen hammer.
2. Planish carefully two or three times.
3. Raise the base and planish in a like manner.
4. Level by filing.
5. Make the middle ring, divide it, and file the scallops.
6. Make the base ring.
7. Remove the center section of the base shell.
8. Fit and solder the different pieces together.

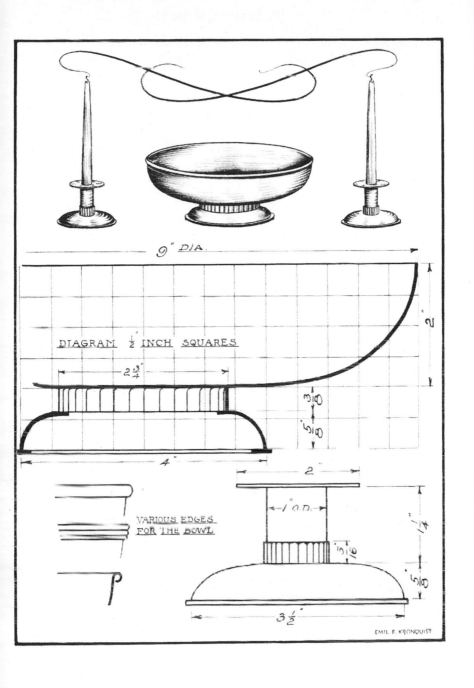

9" DIA.

DIAGRAM ½ INCH SQUARES

2"

2 ¾"

3/8"

5/8"

4"

VARIOUS EDGES
FOR THE BOWL

2"

1" O.D.

5/16"

1 ¼"

5/8"

3 ½"

EMIL F. KRONQUIST

SILENT BUTLER

A handy gadget for emptying ash trays at the bridge table, and at the same time a pretty piece of metalcraft.

Material

Copper.
Aluminum, soft.

Measurements

One circular disk, 7 inches in diameter, No. 18 gauge, Brown and Sharpe, copper; No. 12, if made of aluminum.

One piece, 6 by 6¾ inches, for the lid, No. 18 gauge, Brown and Sharpe, copper; No. 12, if made of aluminum.

One piece, ⅛ by 1 by 4½ inches, for the lift.

One piece, ⅛ by 1 by 5 inches, for the handle.

Six rivets, round head, ³⁄₁₆ by ¼ inch.

Procedure to Be Followed in Making

1. Planish the metal.
2. Anneal and straighten.
3. Prepare a forming block of hardwood, and another for backing (Fig. 1).
4. Clinch the circular disk between the wood, using a vise or clamps.
5. File or cut the handle and the lift to shape. Center punch and drill the holes (Figs. 2 and 3).
6. Cut the lid to shape using a jeweler's saw for the hinge (Fig. 4).
7. Make the hinge (Figs. 5 and 6).
8. Fit and rivet the different parts together.

In raising the edge of the container over the circular wood form, the metal should be annealed a few times. It is a good deal of metal to crowd in and it must be done in easy stages.

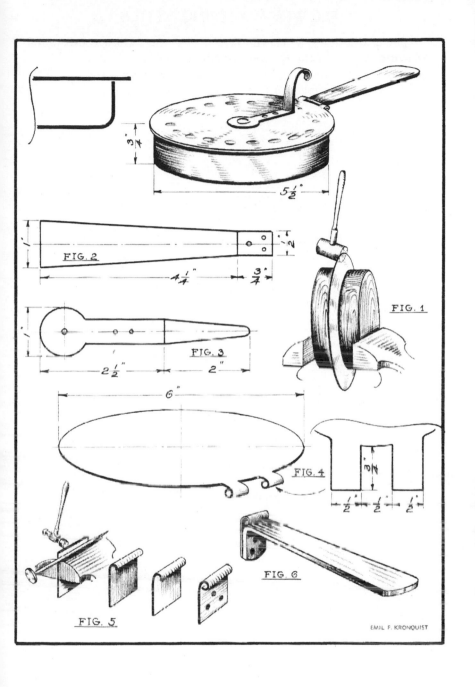

FIG. 2

FIG. 1

FIG. 3

FIG. 4

FIG. 6

FIG. 5

EMIL F. KRONQUIST

FLOWER WATERING KETTLE

This attractive project was sketched at the Paris Exposition of Arts and Crafts, in the German pavilion. The principal dimensions are shown in the drawing but the details must be worked out. The wood is ebony or teak. All joints are hard soldered.

Material

Copper or brass.
Silver.

Measurements

One disk, 11 inches in diameter, No. 18 gauge, Brown and Sharpe.
One disk, 8¼ inches in diameter, No. 18.
One disk, 2¾ inches, No. 18.
Two strips, ¼ by 7½ inches, No. 18.
One piece, 6½ by 8 inches, No. 18. Spout.
Hinges made from ⅛- by ½-inch rectangular stock.

Procedure to Be Followed in Making

1. Make a template for the curvature of the bowl (Fig. 1).
2. Raise the bowl. (See page 14, *Raising*.)
3. Planish carefully two or three times. Anneal and pickle the metal between each planishing.
4. Make the different parts for the cover and the lid.
5. Make the fittings for the hinges.
6. Solder.
7. Make the spout.
8. Solder the spout to the kettle.
9. Make the wood fittings.

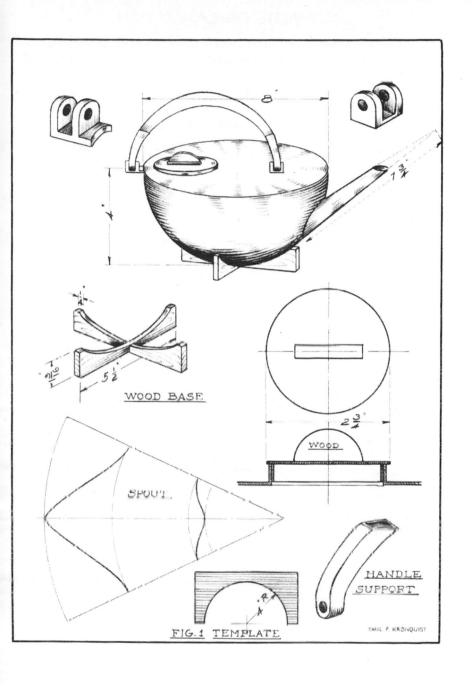

WOOD BASE

WOOD

SPOUT

HANDLE
SUPPORT

EMIL F. KRONQUIST

FIG. 1 TEMPLATE

COMPOTE OR CANDY DISH

A pretty piece of metalcraft which any amateur should be delighted to make. Pewter is suggested because, first, it is a beautiful metal, and second, it is easy to work. The little sea horses can be cut and filed to shape from stock about ¼ inch thick. For the more ambitious, it may be modeled and then cast. A template, as shown in Fig. 1, should be made from stiff manila paper.

Material

Pewter.
Silver.

Measurements (Pewter)

One piece, 5 by 8¾ inches, No. 16 gauge, Brown and Sharpe.
One piece, 2¼ by 3¼ inches, No. 16.
Two balls, ⅜ inch in diameter (from the five-and-ten store).
If made in silver, the gauge of the metal should be No. 18.

Procedure to Be Followed in Making (Pewter)

1. Cut the corners off the metal so that it approximates the shape of the bowl.
2. Planish carefully with a highly polished planishing hammer.
3. Sink it to shape, with a leather-covered mallet, in the hollow of a piece of wood.
4. Replanish on a stake, if necessary.
5. Mark the correct and finished shape to the edges.
6. Saw to the line with a jeweler's saw.
7. Finish the edges with files and emery.
8. Bend the ends to hug the balls (Fig. 2).
9. Solder the base to the bowl, use 50-50 solder.
10. Make the sea horses, fit them to the bowl, and solder.

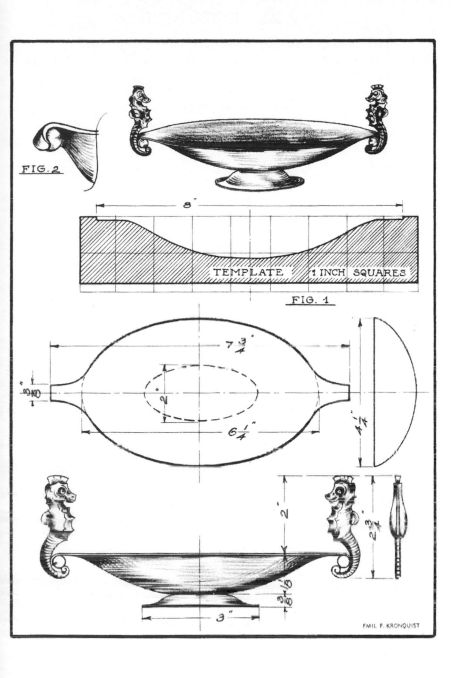

FIG.2

TEMPLATE   1 INCH SQUARES

FIG. 1

EMIL F. KRONQUIST

TABLE CENTER PIECE

Many arrangements are possible with this split, circular ring which can be separated and inverted, or made to form an S. It may be used entirely as a candlestick, or as a combination flower holder and candleholder; a little wax in the bottom of the tubing would make it watertight. Short glass test tubes could also be used.

Many different sizes of diameters, of course, can be made to suit individual taste.

Material

Aluminum, soft.
Brass, soft.

Measurements

One piece, $\frac{3}{8}$ by $1\frac{3}{4}$ by 48 inches (allowance with overlap). Ten pieces of tubing, 1 inch o.d. by $\frac{7}{8}$ inch i.d. by $1\frac{3}{4}$ inches long. Ten 8-32 by $\frac{1}{2}$-inch round-head screws.

Procedure to Be Followed in Making

1. Bend the bar stock around something about 12 inches in diameter. The ring will expand when the pressure is released. Or it may be taken to a sheet-metal shop and rolled to size.
2. Cut the two segments with a hack saw.
3. Center-punch for drilling.
4. Drill and tap for 8-32 screws (Fig. 4).
5. Spread or flare the tubing as shown in Fig. 1. Use any round punch or ball-peen hammer.
6. Shrink the other end of the tubing, starting as shown in Fig. 2 and finishing as shown in Fig. 3.

A pleasing combination could be made by making the ring of aluminum and the holders of brass or bronze.

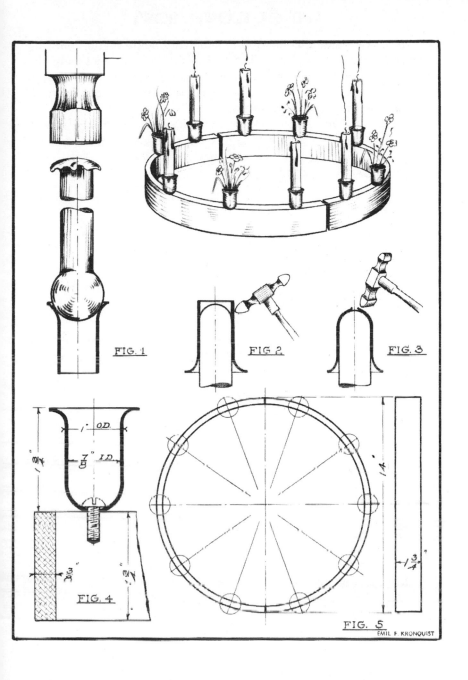

FIG. 1

FIG 2

FIG. 3

FIG. 4

1" O.D.

7" I.D.
8

1 3"
4

3"

1 3"
4

FIG. 5

4"

1 3"
4

EMIL F. KRONQUIST

FRUIT OR FLOWER BOWL

An artistic ensemble made in yellow and white metal. This design is a modification of one sketched in the Danish pavilion of the Paris Exposition of Modern Arts and Crafts. The bowl and the support are made in aluminum. The four scrolls are made in brass or bronze. The rivets are aluminum.

A full-size working drawing should be made from the sketch shown in Fig. 1. All necessary dimensions are given. Study the ingenious way all the pieces are put together without soldering (with the exception of tacking the scrolls).

Material

Aluminum and brass.

Measurements

One aluminum disk, 13 inches in diameter, No. 12 gauge, Brown and Sharpe.

One aluminum disk, 7 inches in diameter, No. 14.

One rectangular brass strip, $\frac{3}{32}$ by 1 by 32 inches.

Two rectangular brass strips, $\frac{3}{32}$ by $\frac{3}{4}$ by 10 inches.

One aluminum rivet, round head, $\frac{1}{4}$ by $\frac{3}{8}$ inch.

Four aluminum rivets, round head, $\frac{1}{8}$ by $\frac{3}{8}$ inch.

Procedure to Be Followed in Making

1. Raise the bowl. (See *Shallow Hollowing*, page 10.)
2. Raise the base.
3. Spread the ends of the brass strips to the sizes shown in the drawings.
4. File and true up the strips, then anneal.
5. Form the scrolls.
6. Fit them together; drill the holes.
7. Rivet and solder the scrolls together (Fig. 2).
8. Notch the base (Fig. 3).
9. Drill the three holes in the bowl.
10. Rivet all the pieces together.

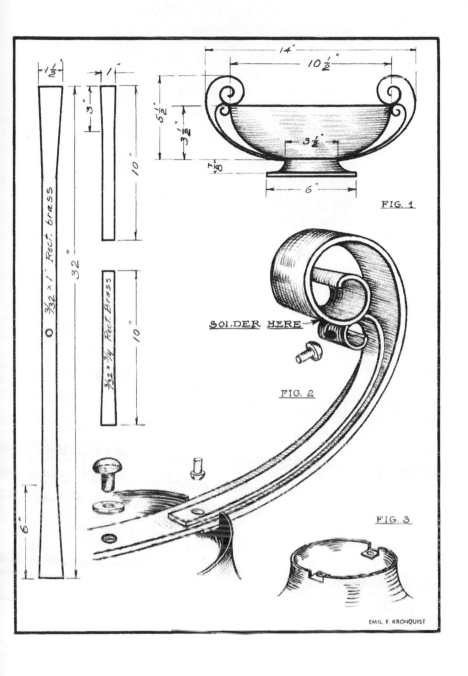

$1\frac{1}{32}$"

$\frac{3}{32}$ × 1" Rect. brass

32"

6"

1"

3"

10"

$\frac{3}{32}$ × $\frac{3}{4}$ Rect. Brass

10"

14"

$10\frac{1}{2}$"

$5\frac{1}{2}$"

$3\frac{1}{2}$"

$3\frac{1}{2}$"

$\frac{7}{8}$"

6"

FIG. 1

SOLDER HERE

FIG. 2

FIG. 3

EMIL F. KRONQUIST

TWO-LIGHT CANDLESTICK

For the craftworker who has a lathe and the ambition to do a little chasing, this would be an interesting project. Pewter, brass, and silver can be turned on any wood-turning lathe and with the same kinds of tools as for turning wood.

The base as shown would have to be filled with pitch and set up on a pitch bowl so that the decorative line work could be chased; however, the base may be left a plain planished dome.

Material

Pewter.
Copper.
Silver.

Measurements (Pewter)

Base, 4 by 6 inches, No. 16 gauge, Brown and Sharpe.
Lower base ring, $\frac{3}{8}$ by 14 inches, No. 14.
Outer scroll, $\frac{3}{4}$ by $8\frac{3}{4}$ inches, No. 12.
Inner scroll, $\frac{3}{4}$ by $6\frac{1}{2}$ inches, No. 12.
Candleholders, 1 inch o.d. tubing, $\frac{1}{16}$-inch wall, $1\frac{1}{4}$ inches long.
Drip cups, $1\frac{3}{4}$ inches in diameter, No. 16.
Stems, $2\frac{1}{2}$ inches, turned from $\frac{1}{2}$-inch round stock.
Center finial, $2\frac{1}{2}$ inches, turned from $\frac{7}{8}$-inch round stock.

When made in copper or silver, the base and candleholders should be No. 18 gauge metal.

Procedure to Be Followed in Making

1. Shape the base.
2. Shape, fit, and solder the lower base ring to the base.
3. Flare the ends of the scrolls, then bend to the proper shape.
4. Shape the tubing.
5. Make the cups.
6. Solder the candleholders to the drip cups.
7. Turn the stems.
8. Turn the finial.
9. Fit the different members.
10. Solder together.

The base must be chased before final assembly.

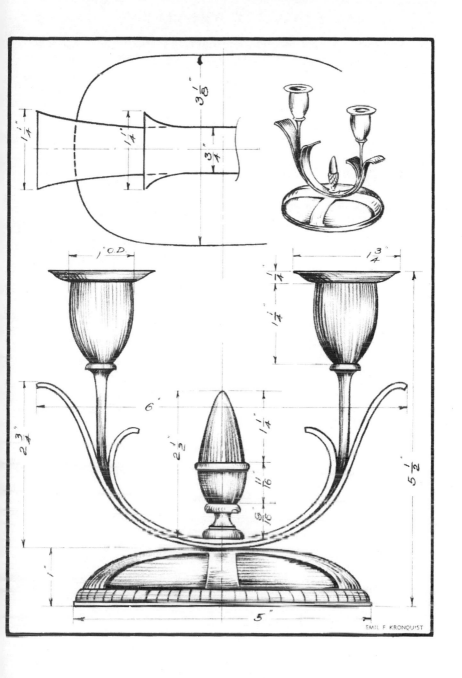

3⅛"

3¾"

1¼"

1¼"

1" O.D.

1¾"

¼"

1¼"

6"

1¼"

2½"

2¾"

11/16"

9/16"

5½"

1"

5"

EMIL F. KRONQUIST

NOVELTY ASH TRAY

The mechanically inclined can have fun making this little ash container and it is a rather nice piece of work when finished.

Material

Copper.
Brass.
Aluminum.

Measurements

One piece $\frac{3}{16}$-inch square wire, 12 inches long.
One piece No. 18 round wire, 12 inches long.
One circular disk, 3 inches in diameter, $\frac{1}{8}$ inch thick.
One circular disk, 3 inches in diameter, No. 18 gauge.
One circular disk, $2\frac{3}{4}$ inches in diameter, No. 18 gauge.
All other dimensions as shown in the drawing.

Procedure to Be Followed in Making

1. Coil the square wire around a piece of cold-rolled steel $2\frac{1}{2}$ inches in diameter (Fig. 3).
2. Cut the required section.
3. Raise the bowl and the base with the ball-peen hammer, then planish.
4. Cut the lower disk.
5. Make the smaller fittings.
6. Make the wire hangers.
7. Finish the parts before assembly.

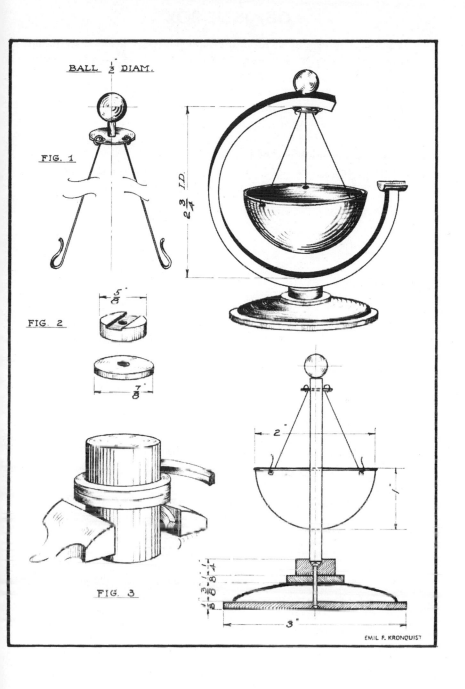

BALL ½" DIAM.

FIG. 1

FIG. 2

FIG. 3

2 ¾" I.D.

⅝"

⅞"

2"

3"

EMIL F. KRONQUIST

CIGARETTE BOX

A popular item and a charming one. A great variety of applied ornamentation can be soldered on to the cover. Brass and pewter make a pleasing combination of color.

A piece of metal can be scored, very much like a piece of cardboard, so that a sharp bend may be made. Use a blunt chisel with an edge filed to an approximate angle of 90 degrees, and a small hammer (Fig. 1). In laying out the measurements, allowance must be made for the thickness of the metal.

A great many different borders can be made on the edge of a piece of metal by using different shaped chasing tools or punches (Fig. 2).

Material

Pewter and brass.

Measurements

One piece, $1\frac{1}{4}$ by $14\frac{5}{16}$ inches, No. 14 gauge, Brown and Sharpe.
Two pieces, $3\frac{1}{4}$ by $4\frac{1}{4}$ inches, No. 14 gauge, Brown and Sharpe.
Four pieces, $\frac{1}{4}$ by $1\frac{1}{2}$ inches, No. 14 gauge, Brown and Sharpe.

Procedure to Be Followed in Making

1. Remove all blemishes with fine pumice powder and water; rub in one direction only.
2. Lay out, with the try square and a scratch awl, the lines necessary for scoring and beveling (Fig. 1).
3. Bevel the ends with a file to an angle of 45 degrees.
4. Score the metal.
5. Bend the frame and solder (Fig. 3).
6. Wash and adjust the frame.
7. Hammer the edges of the top and bottom, as shown in Fig. 2.
8. Solder the frame to the bottom (Fig. 4).
9. Make the corner pieces and solder them to the lid (Fig. 5).
10. Make the decorative units and solder to the cover.

Soldering pewter is explained on page 30.

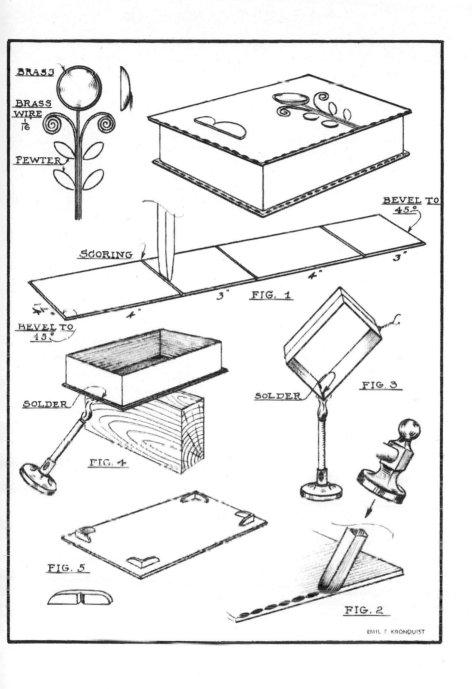

BRASS

BRASS
WIRE
$\frac{1}{16}$

PEWTER

BEVEL TO
45°

SCORING

3"   4"   3"

4"   FIG. 1

BEVEL TO
45°

SOLDER

FIG. 4

FIG. 3

SOLDER

FIG. 5

FIG. 2

EMIL F. KRONQUIST

THREE-LIGHT CANDLESTICK

Copper and brass or aluminum and brass make pleasing combinations. This three-light candlestick is attractive in either one of the combinations.

Material

Copper and brass.
Aluminum and brass.

Measurements

The measurements are given on the sketches. It will be noted that the base size is the same in all four designs, but the length of the stock for the scroll and candleholders varies.

Procedure to Be Followed in Making

1. Flare or spread the ends of the scroll to about $1\frac{1}{2}$ inches, then planish the whole length.
2. Anneal, pickle, and straighten.
3. Lay out a full-size drawing of the curve of the scroll.
4. Bend the metal by careful hammering.
5. Cut, flare, fit, and soft-solder the candleholders to the scroll. The solder should be placed on the inside of the tubing.
6. Drill and countersink the holes to receive the rivets (Fig. 5).
7. File and finish the $\frac{1}{4}$ by $1\frac{1}{2}$ by 12-inch brass bar.
8. Assemble.

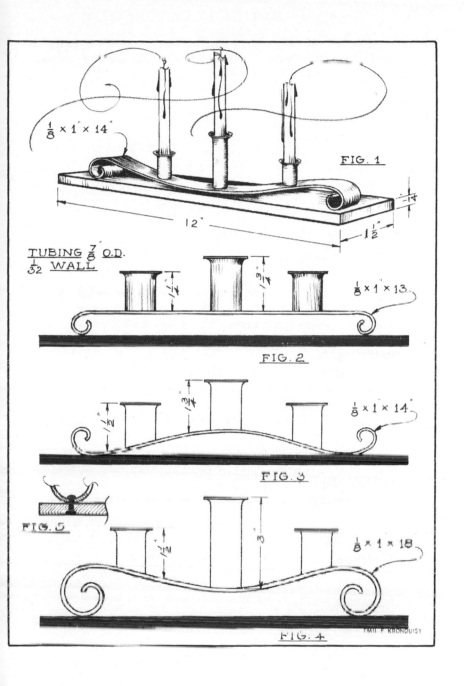

$\frac{1}{8} \times 1" \times 14"$

FIG. 1

12"

$1\frac{1}{2}"$

$\frac{1}{4}$

TUBING $\frac{7}{8}$ O.D.
$\frac{1}{32}$ WALL

$\frac{1}{2}"$ $1\frac{3}{4}"$

$\frac{1}{8} \times 1" \times 13"$

FIG. 2

$1\frac{3}{4}"$ $\frac{1}{2}"$

$\frac{1}{8} \times 1" \times 14"$

FIG. 3

FIG. 5

$1\frac{1}{4}"$ $3"$

$\frac{1}{8} \times 1" \times 18"$

FIG. 4

EMIL F KRONQUIST

10-INCH TRAY

This tray was designed primarily as an exercise for students interested in art metalwork. It is well within the scope of work a beginner may attempt. It is pleasing in proportion and good looking when finished.

Material

Copper, soft cold-rolled.

Measurements

Circular disk, 10 inches in diameter; the sunken center, $6\frac{1}{2}$ inches.

Procedure to Be Followed in Making

1. Scrub the metal clean with a scouring compound and water. Rinse and dry.
2. Planish the disk. Choose the best side of the metal and do not strike too hard. Fine planishing looks the best.
3. Anneal and pickle the metal. Rinse and dry.
4. Straighten the metal on a clean smooth iron with a rawhide mallet.
5. Describe the $6\frac{1}{2}$-inch circle with a pair of dividers.
6. Fasten a hardwood block (birch or maple) in the vise with the end grain up.
7. Place two small wire nails in the wood block for a guide, as shown in Fig. 1.
8. Start hammering lightly with a sinking or tray hammer. The blow of the hammer should land where the circular scratch mark is tangent to the edge of the wood (Fig. 1).
9. Two suggestions for finishing the edge are shown in Figs. 3 and 4.

For additional practice, this plate may be etched with a border or center design. (See page 48, *Etching of Metals*.)

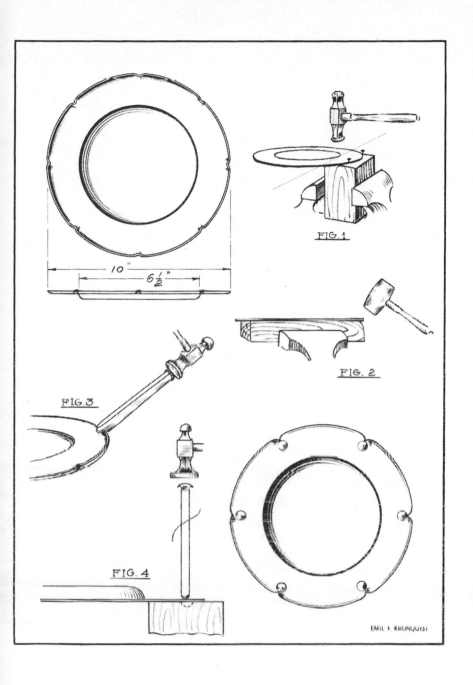

10"

6½"

FIG. 1

FIG. 2

FIG. 3

FIG. 4

EMIL F. KRONQUIST

CANDLE SNUFFER

A novelty which is fun to make and to which a great many variations and individual touches can be applied so as to make it personal. The snuffer part can be made with a broader rim to look like a dunce's cap, or it may be made like a cavalier's chapeau with a long feather as a handle.

Material

Copper or brass.
Pewter with brass handle.
Aluminum.
Silver.

Measurements

One piece 2 by $3\frac{3}{4}$ inches, No. 20 gauge, Brown and Sharpe.
One piece $\frac{1}{8}$ inch square wire, 12 inches long.
Two rivets, $\frac{1}{8}$ by $\frac{1}{4}$ inch, round head.

Procedure to Be Followed in Making

1. Planish the sheet metal to give it a hammered effect.
2. Lay out the snuffer with a divider and cut it to size.
3. Bend the metal to a cone shape and tie it with iron binding wire (Fig. 1). (If riveted as shown in Fig. 2, this is not necessary.)
4. Hard-solder the joint, pickle, and straighten.
5. Wave the edge (Fig. 3).
6. Twist the square wire (Fig. 5).
7. Flatten one end and fit it to the snuffer.
8. Shape the opposite end.
9. Drill the holes for the rivets.
10. Rivet the handle to the snuffer.

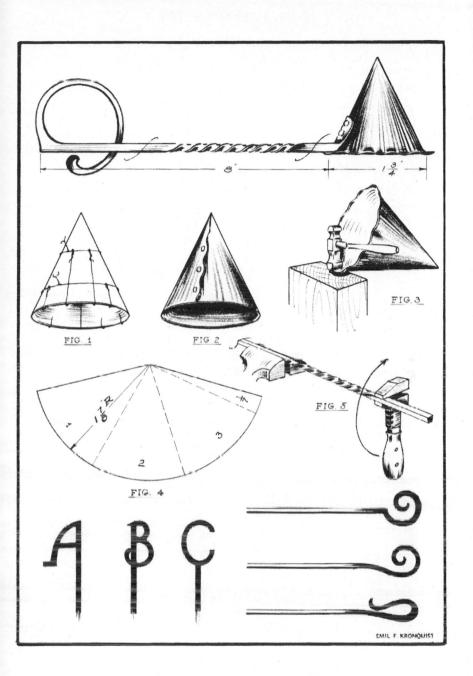

FIG. 1

FIG. 2

FIG. 3

FIG. 4

FIG. 5

A　B　C

EMIL F. KRONQUIST

16-INCH FLUTED TRAY

A popular size of tray that is useful and attractive for serving hors d'oeuvres or other appetizers.

Material

Copper or brass.
Aluminum.
Pewter.

Measurements

Soft aluminum, 16 inches in diameter, No. 12 gauge, Brown and Sharpe.
Pewter, 16 inches in diameter, No. 14.
Copper or brass, soft cold-rolled, 16 inches in diameter, No. 18.

Procedure to Be Followed in Making

1. Clean the metal by scrubbing it with fine pumice powder and water.
2. Select the best side of the metal for the top side.
3. Planish carefully with a hammer having a mirror polish.
4. Soften the metal by annealing. (Pewter cannot be annealed but it can be softened by heating it to approximately 350°F.)
5. Cut the disk to a saucerlike shape with a leather-covered mallet on a sandbag.
6. Smooth out the bumps with a rawhide mallet on a slightly curved stake.
7. With a pair of dividers describe a circle 6 inches in diameter, the size of the well.
8. Sink the center with a tray hammer.
9. Divide the circumference into 16 equal parts and draw radial lines to the center.
10. Prepare a hardwood block with a groove (end grain).
11. Flute the plate as shown in Fig. 1.
12. Turn the center portion of the scallops slightly upward (Fig. 1).
13. File and finish the edge of the metal with emery cloth.

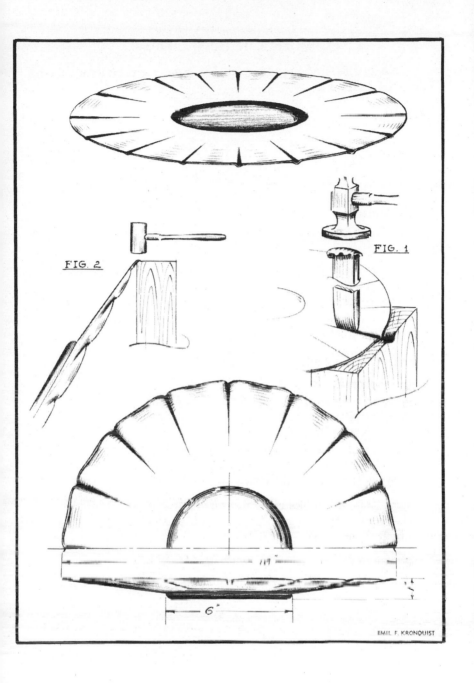

FIG. 2

FIG. 1

11"

6"

EMIL F. KRONQUIST

POWDER OR TRINKET BOX

A box of this kind may be varied in size to accommodate some particular keepsake.

Material

Pewter.
Copper.
Brass.
Silver.

Measurements

Two circular disks, $3\frac{1}{2}$ inches in diameter, No. 18 gauge, Brown and Sharpe; No. 14 for pewter.

One piece, $1\frac{1}{4}$ by 10 inches, No. 18 gauge, Brown and Sharpe; No. 14 for pewter.

One strip for the rim, $\frac{1}{4}$ by 10 inches, No. 18 gauge, Brown and Sharpe.

Scraps of stock for the finial or lift.

Procedure to Be Followed in Making

For copper, brass, or silver:
1. Clean the metal by scrubbing; then planish.
2. Hard-solder the ring. Pickle to remove borax.
3. Finish the joint. Replanish.
4. File, fit, and hard-solder the cylinder to the base.
5. Make the rim to fit the box and hard-solder to the lid.
6. Make the finial and solder to the lid.

When this box is made in pewter, all joints are soft-soldered.

The edges of the top and the bottom may be enriched by a hammered effect; or filed into scallops uniformly spaced; or in units of two, three, or four.

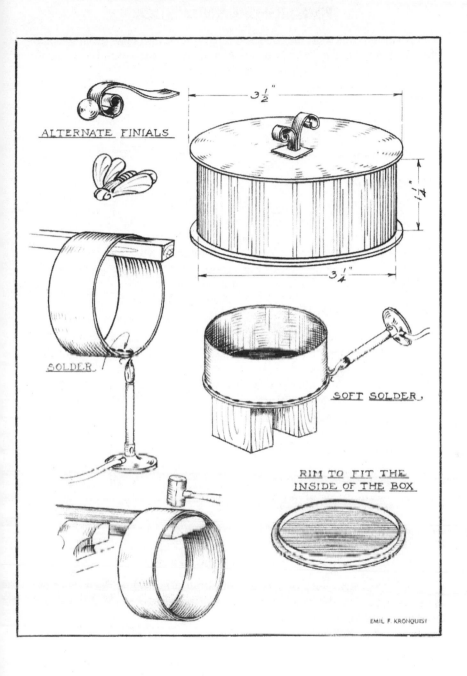

ALTERNATE FINIALS

$3\frac{1}{2}''$

$1\frac{1}{4}''$

$3\frac{1}{4}''$

SOLDER

SOFT SOLDER.

RIM TO FIT THE
INSIDE OF THE BOX

EMIL F. KRONQUIST

FIVE-LIGHT CANDLESTICK

A candlestick that can be used singly or in pairs for table decoration or over the fireplace. It may be made for three lights by shortening the length of the supporting bar to 22 inches.

Material

Copper.
Brass.
Aluminum.

Measurements

One rectangular bar, $\frac{1}{8}$ by $1\frac{1}{4}$ by 28 inches.
Two pieces, $\frac{1}{8}$ by $\frac{5}{8}$ by $3\frac{1}{2}$ inches, for the feet.
Five stems, $\frac{1}{4}$-inch round stock, $2\frac{3}{8}$ inches long.
Five candle *bobêches*, 2 inches in diameter, No. 18 gauge.
Five candleholders, $1\frac{1}{4}$ inches long, $\frac{7}{8}$ inch o.d., $\frac{1}{16}$-inch wall.
Two $\frac{3}{16}$-inch round-head rivets, $\frac{3}{8}$ inch long.

Procedure to Be Followed in Making

1. Spread the ends of the rectangular bar by hammering (Fig. 1). Then planish the entire strip of metal. Anneal, pickle, and straighten.
2. Lay out a full-size drawing of curvature, using a piece of wire 28 inches long as a guide to the limit of the length.
3. Center-punch the middle of the bar.
4. Form the scrolls; begin as shown in Fig. 2A, then B, C, and D.
5. Planish and spread the candleholder (Fig. 3).
6. Taper the stems by hammering; then file the shoulders, leaving pegs about $\frac{1}{8}$ inch in diameter.
7. Solder the candleholders to the cups.
8. Drill holes and rivet the candleholders to the cups.
9. Drill and fit the stems to the main scroll and rivet (Fig. 4).
10. Shape, drill, and rivet the feet in place.

When this candlestick is made in aluminum and soldering is not possible, the candleholders can be made as shown in the corner sketch and riveted in place.

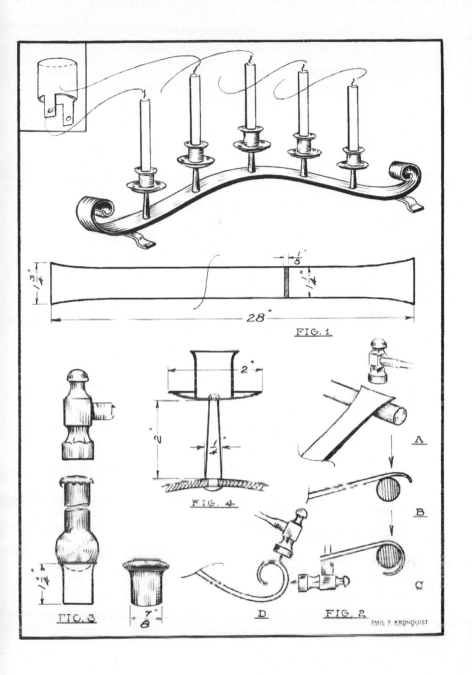

FIG. 1

FIG. 4

FIG. 3

FIG. 2

EMIL F. KRONQUIST

READING OR STUDY LAMP

An interesting piece of work for the person with a little mechanical ingenuity. It is simple to make and good looking when finished.

Material

Copper.
Brass or bronze.

Measurements

Circular disk for base, 8 inches in diameter, No. 18 gauge, Brown and Sharpe.

Candle cup, $3\frac{1}{2}$ inches in diameter, No. 18 gauge, Brown and Sharpe.

Candleholder, $1\frac{1}{2}$ inches o.d. tubing, $\frac{1}{16}$-inch wall, 2 inches long.

Supporting arm, $\frac{1}{8}$ by $\frac{5}{8}$ by 13 inches.

Upright, $\frac{1}{2}$-inch square tubing, $\frac{1}{16}$-inch wall, 16 inches long. (This upright may be made from round tubing, which simplifies construction.)

Shade, $7\frac{1}{2}$ by 15 inches, No. 24 gauge.

The shade and arm supports can be made from tubing of a size that telescopes the upright.

Procedure to Be Followed in Making

1. Cut all the required stock.
2. Scrub it clean and give it a hammered or planished surface texture.
3. Make the base (Figs. 1, 2, and 3).
4. Draw the shape of the arm full size and bend it to the shape of the diagram (Fig. 4).
5. Make the upright. Twist as shown in Fig. 5.
6. Make the fittings.
7. Make the shade (Fig. 7).
8. Assemble.

The electric wiring can be done in several ways, either exposed or concealed, and a canopy switch may be placed in the base.

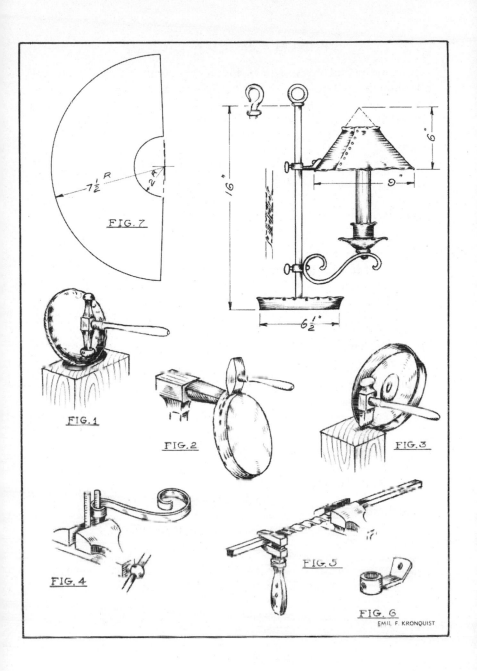

FIG. 7

FIG. 1

FIG. 2

FIG. 3

FIG. 4

FIG. 5

FIG. 6

EMIL F. KRONQUIST

PUNCH OR SOUP LADLE

An individual touch may be given this piece of work by the application of a monogram or letter. The handle is made from a rectangular piece of stock and spread by hammering. The bowl is raised, as shown on page 12.

Material

Copper.
Silver.

Measurements

One rectangular bar, $\frac{3}{16}$ by $\frac{1}{2}$ by 11 inches; the metal will stretch by hammering.
One circular disk, $5\frac{1}{2}$ inches, No. 18 gauge, Brown and Sharpe.
One piece, 1 by 4 inches, No. 22, for applied ornament.
Three round-head rivets, $\frac{1}{8}$ by $\frac{1}{4}$ inch.
Six round-head rivets, $\frac{1}{16}$ by $\frac{1}{8}$ inch.

Procedure to Be Followed in Making

1. Forge the rectangular bar to the dimensions shown in Fig. 1; then anneal.
2. Planish the metal carefully.
3. Cut it to shape with the jeweler's saw; file the edges and finish with emery cloth.
4. Raise the circular disk to the required size.
5. Planish the bowl (Fig. 2).
6. Make the spout (Fig. 3).
7. Finish the edge by filing.
8. Bend and fit the handle to the bowl.
9. Fit and rivet the ornament to the handle.
10. Fit and rivet the handle to the bowl.

The spreading and hammering of the handle may be done on any good-sized piece of steel, not necessarily an anvil as shown.

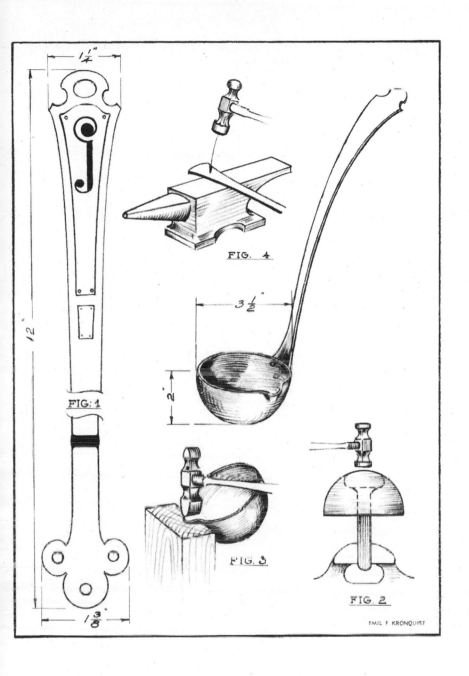

1¼"

12"

FIG. 1

1⅜"

FIG. 4

3½"

2"

FIG. 3

FIG. 2

EMIL F. KRONQUIST

SERVING TRAY

A popular size of tray that can be made with very few tools. It lends itself to a decorative motif for etching.

Material

One piece of soft aluminum, 10 by 23 inches, No. 12 gauge, Brown and Sharpe.

Procedure to Be Followed in Making

1. Clean the metal by scrubbing with fine pumice powder and water or a kitchen cleanser. Rinse and dry.
2. Planish the entire surface, using a highly polished planishing hammer.
3. Anneal the metal.
4. Straighten with a rawhide mallet.
5. Lay out the various measurements and cut with a jeweler's saw.
6. File all the edges of the metal, then smooth the edges with emery cloth.
7. File a miter joint on the four ½-inch corners.
8. Bend the edges by clamping the metal between two pieces of wood as shown. (If a brake is available, use it.)
9. Curve the handles over a piece of round steel (Fig. 4).

There are many ways the edges of a tray can be finished. Figure 3 has an extra strip of metal applied with "cold solder."

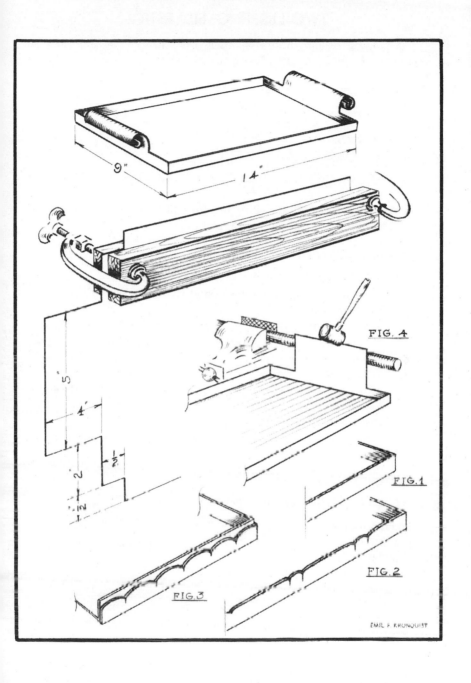

9"

14"

5"

4"

$\frac{1}{2}$"

2"

$\frac{1}{2}$"

FIG. 4

FIG. 1

FIG. 2

FIG. 3

EMIL F. KRONQUIST

TWO-LIGHT CANDLESTICK

A modern design in simple lines. For the center finial can be substituted a piece of cut crystal or colored plastic.

Material

Pewter.

Measurements

One piece, $\frac{3}{10}$ by $\frac{3}{4}$ by 11 inches, for arm.
One circular disk, 4 inches in diameter, No. 14 gauge, Brown and Sharpe.
One piece, $\frac{1}{8}$ by $\frac{3}{8}$ by 12 inches for the base ring.
Other dimensions as shown on the drawing.

Procedure to Be Followed in Making

1. Hollow the 4-inch disk (Figs. 1 and 2).
2. Hollow the two candle cups slightly (Fig. 4).
3. Planish carefully (Fig. 3).
4. Make the lower base ring; fit and solder to the base (Fig. 5).
5. Make candleholders (Fig. 6). (These may be made from tubing having a 1-inch o.d. with a $\frac{1}{16}$-inch wall.)
6. Solder the candleholders to the candle cups.
7. Make the arm. File the stock to shape and sizes, as shown in Fig. 7. A coarse file should be used in roughing to size.
8. Bend it to the desired shape.
9. Make the $1\frac{1}{2}$-inch disk, saw the pewter with an ordinary coping saw. (Pewter can be turned; use regular wood turning tools.)
10. Make the finial.
11. Assemble by soldering the different units together.

Wood patterns could be made of the arm, finial, and circular $1\frac{1}{2}$-inch disk and a plaster of Paris mold made wherein they could be cast (see page 36).

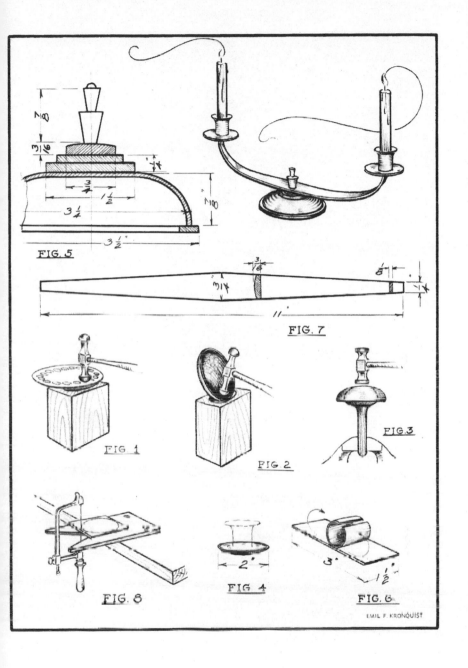

FIG. 5

FIG. 7

FIG 1

FIG 2

FIG.3

FIG. 8

FIG 4

FIG. 6

EMIL F. KRONQUIST

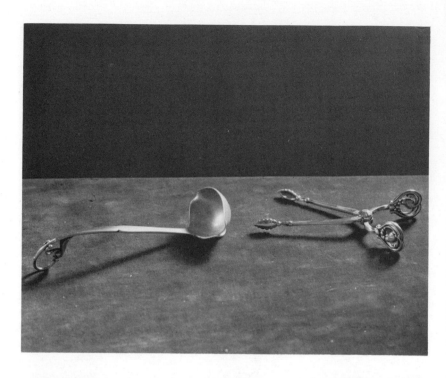

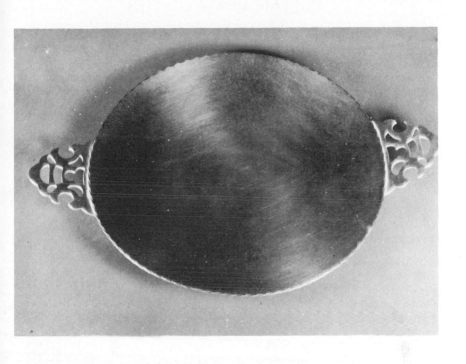

ROMAN LAMP LIGHTER

For the more ambitious craftworker in metal, this project should have appeal. The ornamentation is chased but could be omitted. The cost of making it in silver is not prohibitive, since the lighter is comparatively small in size.

Material

Silver.
Pewter.

Measurements (Silver)

The same as shown in the drawings. The center bowl is raised from a 4½-inch circular disk. All the parts, except the handle and the lower base ring, are made from No. 20 gauge, Brown and Sharpe metal.

When the lamp is made in pewter, the gauge of the metal should be somewhat heavier.

Procedure to Be Followed in Making

1. Raise the pieces, as shown in Figs. 1, 3, and 4.
2. Make the spout (Fig. 5).
3. Make the handle from No. 14 gauge metal (Fig. 2).
4. Make the base ring (Fig. 6).
5. Fit and solder the different members together.
6. Final assembly.

All chasing must be done before final assembly.

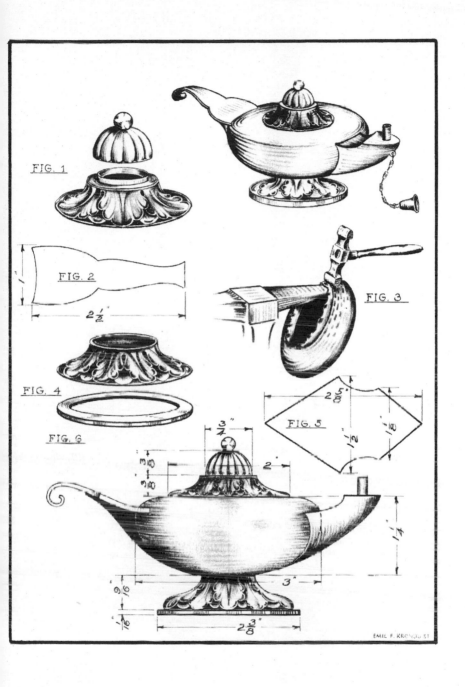

FIG. 1

FIG. 2

$1''$

$2\frac{1}{2}''$

FIG. 3

FIG. 4

FIG. 6

FIG. 5

$2\frac{5}{8}''$

$1\frac{1}{2}''$

$1\frac{1}{8}''$

$\frac{3}{4}''$

$2''$

$\frac{3}{8}''$ $\frac{3}{16}''$

$\frac{3}{8}''$

$1\frac{1}{4}''$

$\frac{9}{16}''$

$3''$

$\frac{1}{16}''$

$2\frac{3}{8}''$

EMIL F. KRONQUIST

SKETCHES OF PROJECTS

THUMBNAIL SKETCHES

The projects on the pages to follow are what may be called "thumbnail sketches" of work which has been made at one time or another. The sources of the designs are unknown; most likely all are recastings of existing designs changed a little here and there to suit the taste of some individual. Some are good and some are not so good, but all could be made excellent if time and study were given to such things as sizes, proportions, curves, and decorations.

The sketches are merely suggestions for further exploration by the person interested in metalcraft. Visit the library and museum and make full use of these treasure islands; few are without some use to the person bent on giving serious attention to a specific subject.

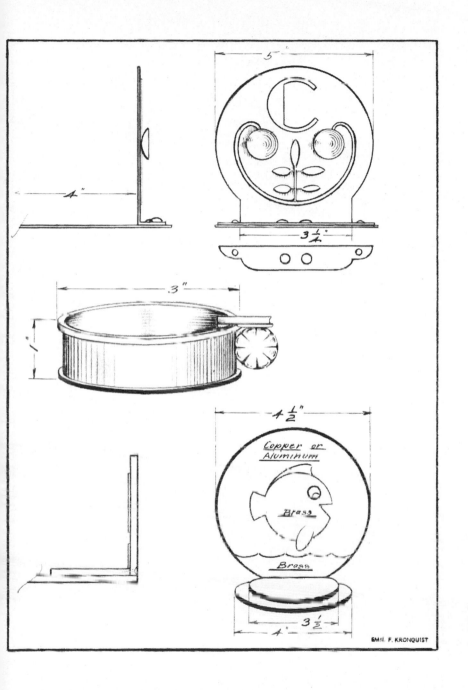

5"

3 1/2"

4"

3"

1"

4 1/2"

Copper or
Aluminum

Brass

Brass

3 1/2"

4"

EMIL. F. KRONQUIST

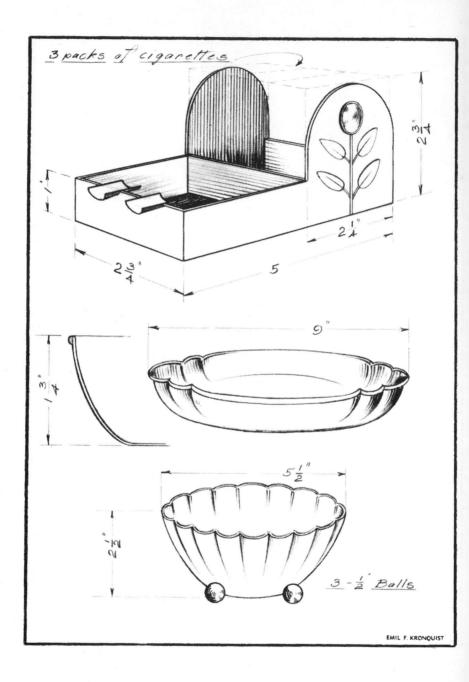

3 packs of cigarettes

$2\frac{3}{4}''$

1"

$2\frac{1}{4}''$

$2\frac{3}{4}''$

5

9"

$1\frac{3}{4}''$

$5\frac{1}{2}''$

$2\frac{1}{2}''$

3 - $\frac{1}{2}''$ Balls

EMIL F. KRONQUIST

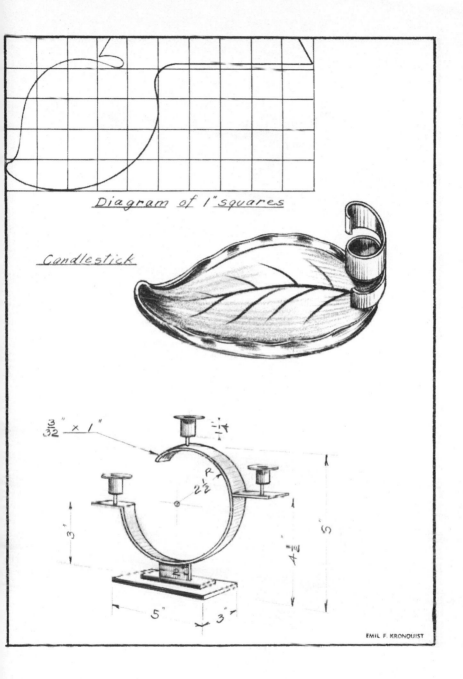

Diagram of 1" squares

Candlestick

$\frac{3}{32}$" × 1"

$\frac{1}{4}$

$2\frac{1}{2}$ R

3"

2"

5"

3"

$4\frac{1}{8}$

5"

EMIL F. KRONQUIST

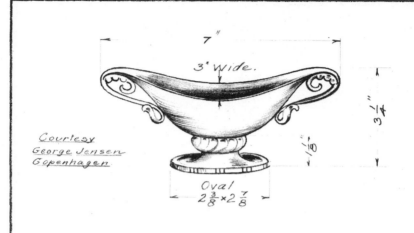

7"

3" wide.

$3\frac{1}{4}$"

$\frac{1}{8}$"

Courtesy
George Jensen
Copenhagen

Oval
$2\frac{3}{8} \times 2\frac{7}{8}$

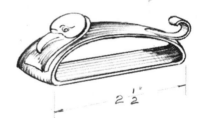

$2\frac{1}{2}$"

Napkin ring

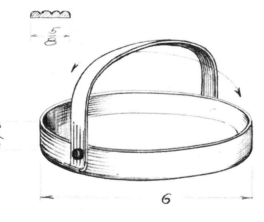

$\frac{5}{8}$

6

EMIL F. KRONQUIST

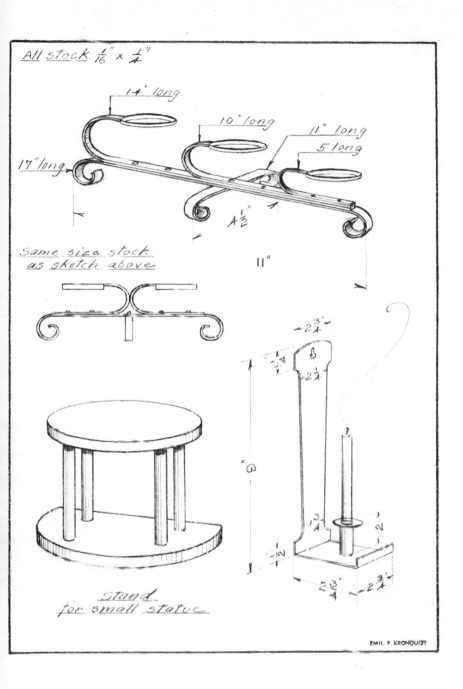

All stock $\frac{1}{16}$" × $\frac{1}{4}$"

14" long

10" long

11" long

5 long

17" long

A $1\frac{1}{2}$"

11"

Same size stock as sketch above

$2\frac{3}{4}$"

$\frac{1}{4}$"

$2\frac{1}{4}$"

$\frac{3}{4}$"

2

G

$\frac{1}{2}$"

$2\frac{3}{4}$"

$2\frac{3}{4}$"

stand
for small statue

EMIL F. KRONQUIST

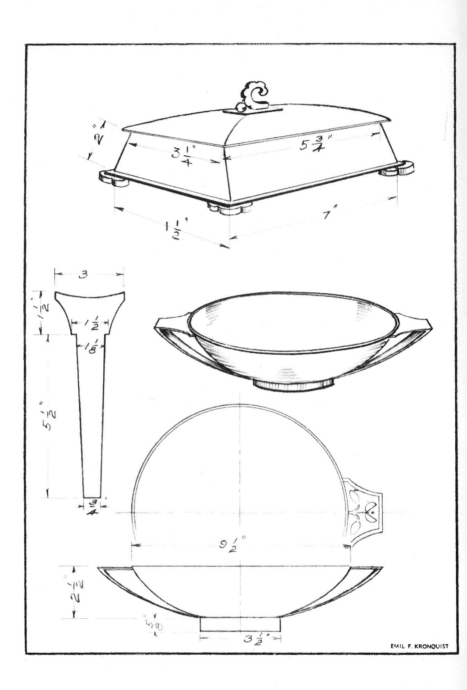

$\frac{1}{4}''$

$\frac{1}{2}''$

$3\frac{1}{4}''$

$5\frac{3}{4}''$

$1\frac{1}{2}''$

$7''$

3

$\frac{1}{2}''$

$1\frac{1}{2}''$

$\frac{1}{8}''$

$5\frac{1}{2}''$

$\frac{3}{4}''$

$9\frac{1}{2}''$

$2\frac{1}{2}''$

$3\frac{1}{2}''$

EMIL F. KRONQUIST

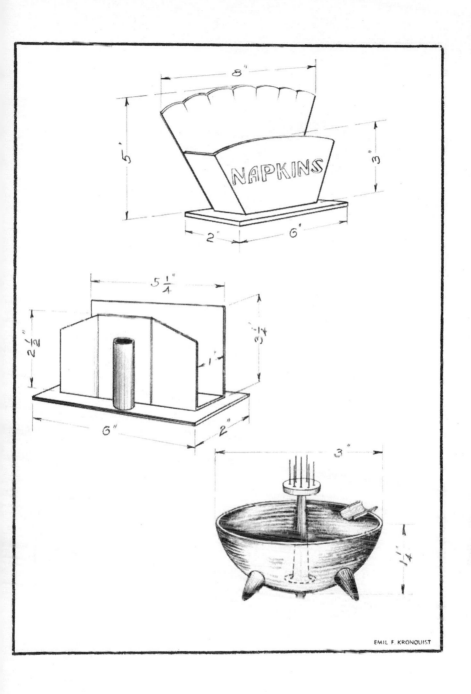

8"

5'

NAPKINS

3"

2"   6"

5 $\frac{1}{4}$"

2 $\frac{1}{2}$"

3 $\frac{1}{4}$"

1"

6"   2"

3"

1 $\frac{1}{4}$"

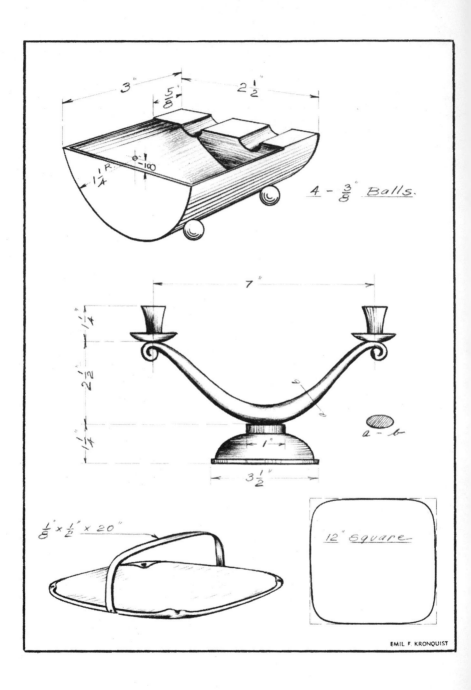

3"   5/8"   2 1/2"

⊕ - 100

1" R.
1/4"

4 - 3/8" Balls.

7"

1 1/4"

2 1/2"

1/4"

1"

3 1/2"

a - b

1/8" x 1/2" x 20"

12" Square

EMIL F. KRONQUIST

Cigarette box

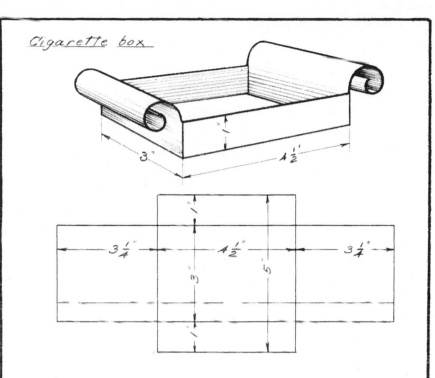

Cigarette box

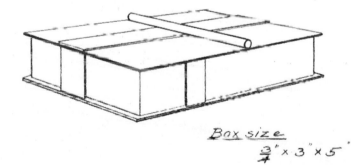

Box size

$\frac{3}{4}" \times 3" \times 5"$

EMIL F. KRONQUIST

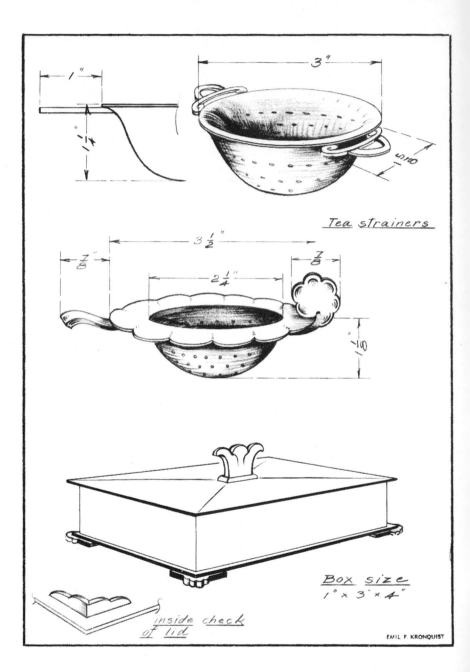

3"

1"

1¼"

⁵⁄₁₀

Tea strainers

3½"

⁷⁄₈"

2¼"

⁷⁄₈"

⁵⁄₁₀"

inside check of lid

Box size
1" × 3" × 4"

EMIL F. KRONQUIST

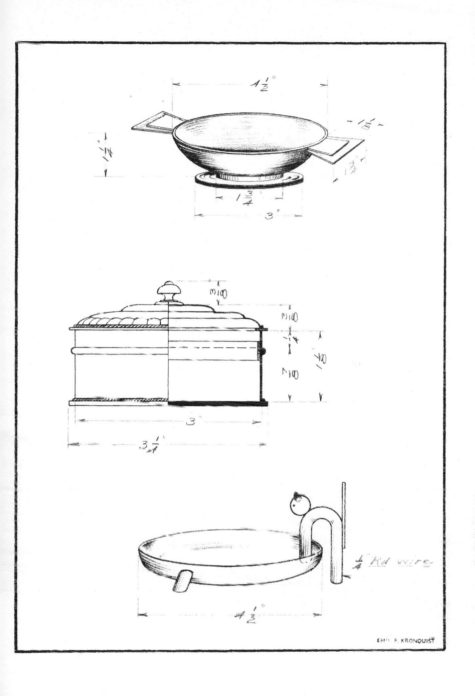

EMIL F. KRONQUIST

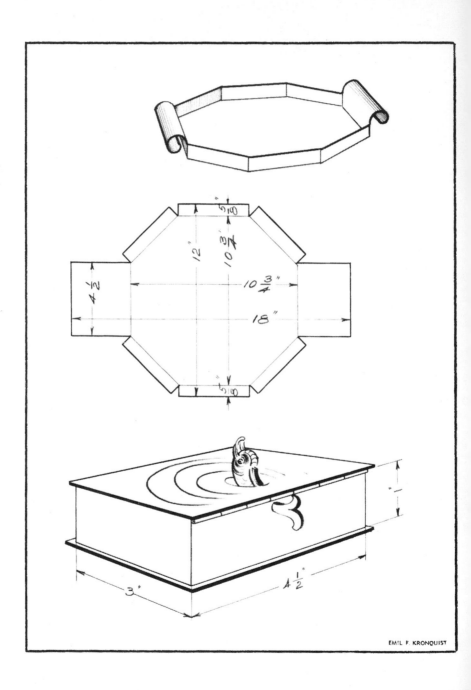

12"

10 3/4"

5/8"

10 3/4"

4 1/2

18"

5/8"

3"

4 1/2"

EMIL F. KRONQUIST

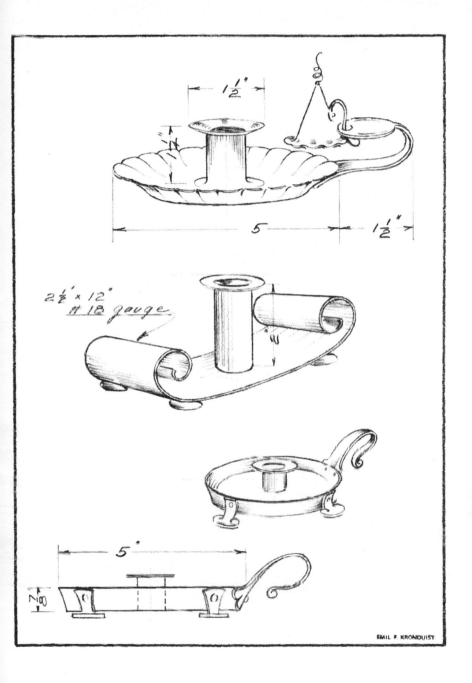

$1\frac{1}{2}''$

$1''$

5'

$1\frac{1}{2}''$

$2\frac{1}{8}'' \times 12''$
#18 gauge

5'

$\frac{7}{8}''$

EMIL F. KRONQUIST

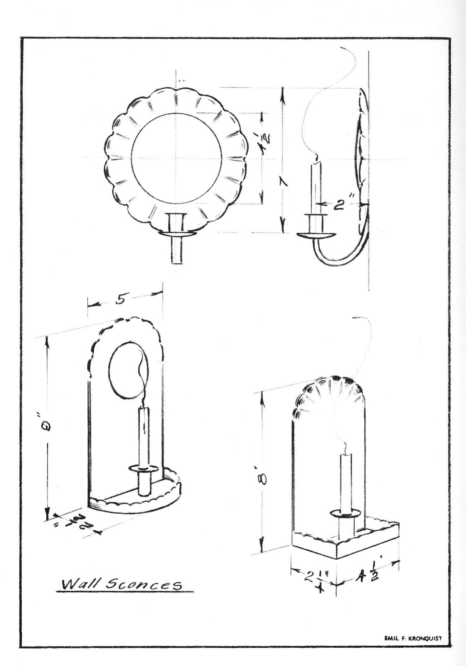

Wall Sconces

EMIL F. KRONQUIST

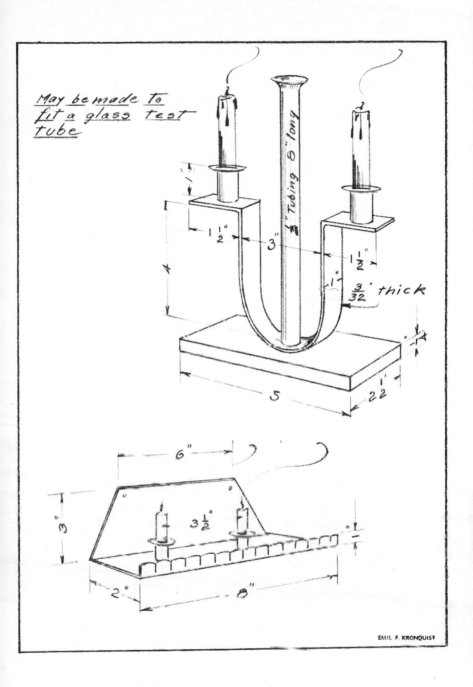

May be made to
fit a glass test
tube

1" Tubing 8" long

1 1/2"

3"

1 1/2"

1"

3/32" thick

4

5

2 1/2"

6"

3"

3 1/2"

2"

8"

EMIL F. KRONQUIST

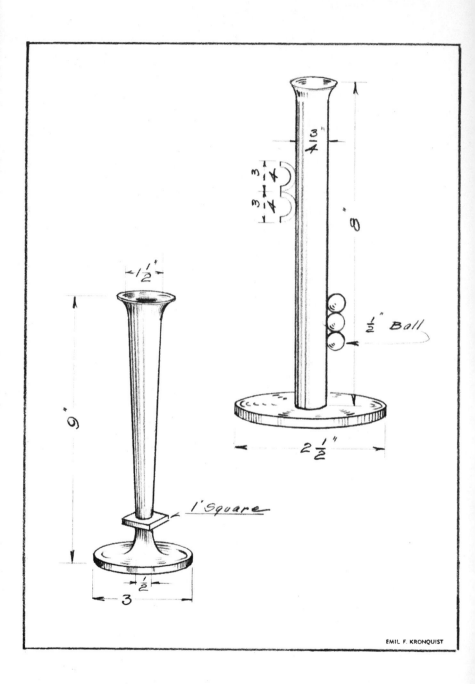

$1\frac{1}{2}''$

$9''$

$1''$ Square

$\frac{1}{2}$

3

$\frac{3}{4}''$

$\frac{3}{4}$

$\frac{3}{4}$

$8''$

$\frac{1}{2}''$ Ball

$2\frac{1}{2}''$

EMIL F. KRONQUIST

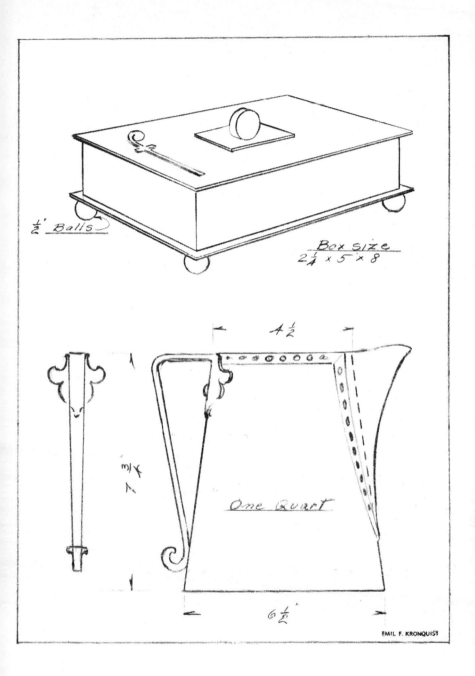

$\frac{1}{2}$' Balls

Box Size
$2\frac{1}{4} \times 5 \times 8$

$4\frac{1}{2}$

$7\frac{3}{4}$"

One Quart

$6\frac{1}{2}$"

EMIL F. KRONQUIST

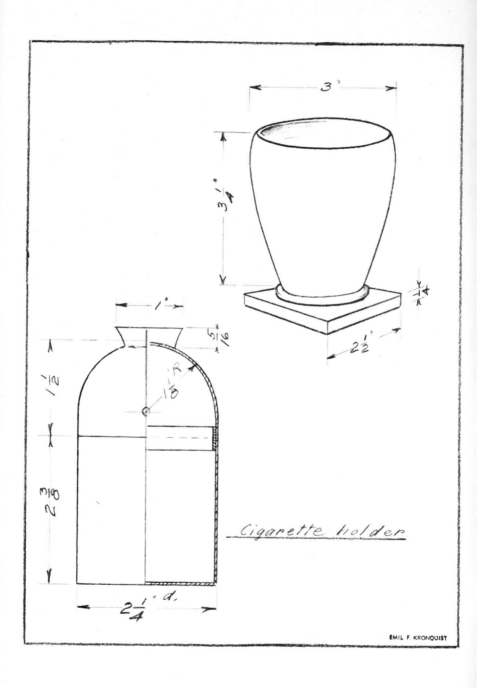

3'

3 1/4"

1/4"

2 1/2'

1"

5/16

1/8 "R

2 1/2'

2 3/8

2 1/4" d.

Cigarette holder

EMIL F. KRONQUIST

May be varied in size for candy, nuts, coasters or cigarettes.

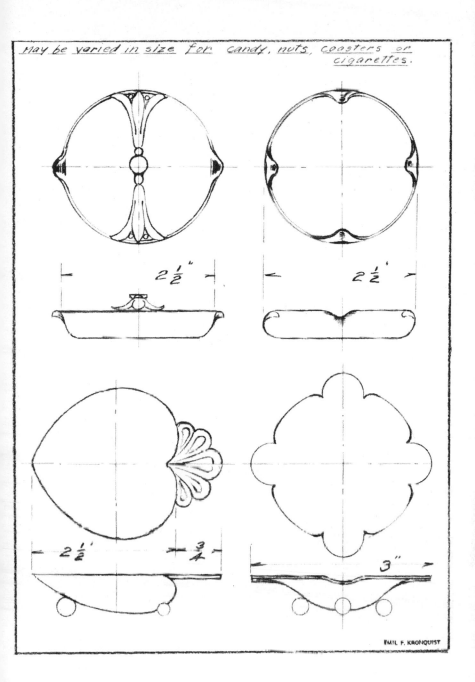

EMIL F. KRONQUIST

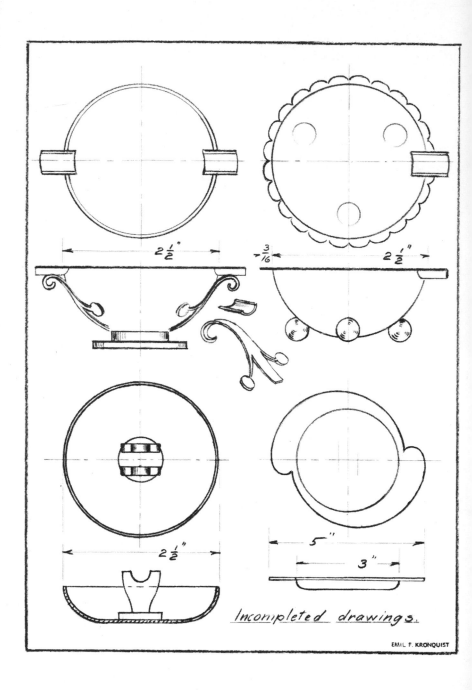

$2\frac{1}{2}''$ $\frac{3}{16}$ $2\frac{1}{2}''$

$2\frac{1}{2}''$ 5″   3″

Incompleted drawings.

EMIL F. KRONQUIST

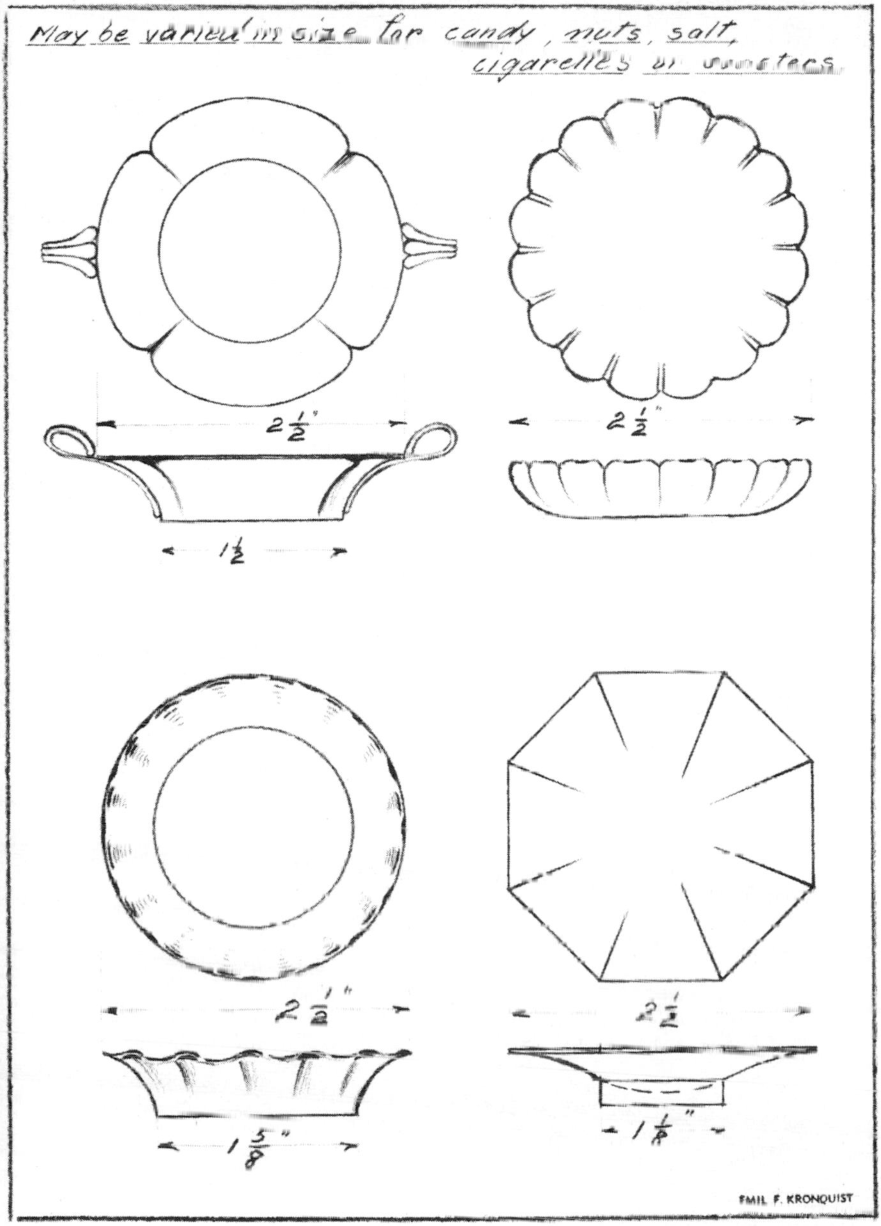

May be varied in size for candy, nuts, salt,
cigarettes or coasters.

$2\frac{1}{2}$"

$1\frac{1}{2}$

$2\frac{1}{2}$"

$2\frac{1}{2}$"

$1\frac{5}{8}$"

$2\frac{1}{2}$"

$1\frac{1}{8}$"

EMIL F. KRONQUIST

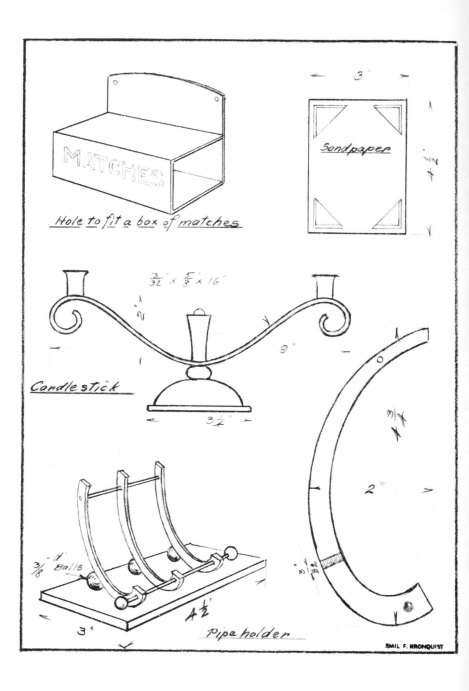

Hole to fit a box of matches

Sandpaper

$3''$

$4\frac{1}{2}''$

MATCHES

Candlestick

$\frac{3}{32}'' \times \frac{5}{8}'' \times 16''$

$2''$

$9''$

$3\frac{1}{4}''$

$\frac{3}{4}''$

$2''$

$\frac{7}{8}''$

Pipe holder

$\frac{3}{8}''d$ Balls

$3''$

$4\frac{1}{2}''$

EMIL F. KRONQUIST

FINISHES ON METALS

FINISHING AND COLORING METALS

There are innumerable ways in which the various metals can be finished and oxidized; different metals require different treatment. Scratches and blemishes should be removed, either with pumice stone or powder, rotten stone, or fine emery cloth. Most work is polished with wheels attached to a lathe, but good work can be done by hand.

Copper and Brass (Natural)

1. Dip the work in the pickling solution for a few minutes.
2. Rinse well in running water.
3. Scrub thoroughly with fine pumice powder and water, rub in one direction only, and do not handle the metal more than necessary.
4. Rinse in hot water and dry with clean rags.
5. Apply a coat of furniture wax and let it dry 15 minutes; then polish with a clean rag.

Oxidizing Copper

1. Dip the work in the pickling solution for a few minutes.
2. Rinse in running water.
3. Scrub thoroughly with a kitchen cleanser or fine pumice powder and water.
4. Mix a solution of liver of sulphur (potassium sulphide) and hot water. Do not make the bath too strong. A pale yellow solution is sufficient and gives a better result.
5. Immerse the work with a whirling motion or up and down for a few seconds.
6. Rinse in running hot water.
7. Dry with a clean rag.
8. Rub the metal surface lightly with dry steel wool No. 0000. High spots should be accentuated by rubbing a little harder.

    If unsuccessful the first time repeat the entire operation, but leave out Steps 1 and 2. Usually a better color is produced in the second dip.
9. Apply a coat of furniture wax and let it dry 15 minutes, then polish with a clean rag.

    For work on which soft solder has been used, a coating of copper can be deposited by immersing the work in an old pickle solution, in which copper has been pickled, so that copper sulphate has formed in the bath. Place a piece of zinc next to the work and hold it in the solution for a couple of

minutes. Iron wires can also be used as either one will pre-
cipitate the copper.

Oxidizing Brass

It is almost impossible to make any prediction as to the color
of brass due to the many different alloys of that metal. The following
formula works well. It is copied from "Chemical Coloring of Metals," by Field and Bonney.

SOLUTION

Arsenious oxide	1 to 2 drams
Hydrochloric acid	2 fluid ounces
Potassium sulphide	½ dram
Water	1 gallon

Dissolve the white arsenic in the acid. Add the solution to the
water, finally adding the liver of sulphur (potassium sulphide).
Use at a temperature of 160°F.

Aluminum. Bright Luster

All aluminum carries a thin stubborn film of oxide, which by
the way is the cause of the difficulty encountered when soldering or
welding the metal; at the same time this film renders excellent protective service.

1. Scrub the metal vigorously with fine pumice powder and
   water; rub in one direction only. (A kitchen cleanser may be
   used in place of pumice.)
2. Rinse in running water to remove all traces of the abrasive
   used. Do not touch the surface of the metal with soiled
   fingers.
3. While still wet, rub the metal with No. 0000 steel wool which
   has previously been rubbed on a cake of ordinary laundry
   soap. This rubbing will produce a lustrous sheen.
4. Rinse in hot running water and dry.
5. Waxing or lacquering is optional.

Aluminum. Mat Finish

1. Prepare a 10 per cent solution of caustic soda (sodium hy-
   droxide) saturated with common salt.
2. Dip the metal for about fifteen seconds.
3. Rinse in running water.
4. Brush the metal with a fine steel scratch brush while wet.
5. Dip again for about thirty seconds.
6. Wash in running hot water and dry.

Pewter

1. Scrub the metal with a fine pumice powder and water.
2. Rinse in running water.
3. While the metal is wet, rub it with No. 0000 steel wool which has been rubbed on a cake of laundry soap.
4. Rinse in hot running water and dry.

   This simple method produces a beautiful silvery luster and a good grade of pewter will retain its luster for a long time.

Silver. Butler Finish

1. Anneal the work and let it cool.
2. Boil it in the pickling solution (sulphuric acid and water) until it becomes pure white.

   The metal may be left in a cold pickling bath for about an hour and the same result will be obtained as by boiling for 1 minute.

   The pickling solution dissolves the extracted deposit of oxide formed in the process of annealing and leaves a coating of fine silver on the surface.
3. Pick up the work with a stick of wood or a copper wire and wash in running water. Do not use iron in any form for picking up the work; it will leave a red deposit on the silver.
4. Scratch-brush the work, using a fine steel wire brush and water. If a revolving brush is used it should run at a very slow speed.
5. Rinse in hot water and dry.

Silver. Oxidized Finish

1. Produce the butler finish first as described.
2. Mix a solution of liver of sulphur and hot water. Do not make the bath too strong; a pale yellow solution is best.
3. Attach the work to a string or a piece of copper or brass wire.
4. Dip the work in boiling water to make it warm.
5. Immerse in the oxidizing bath. Keep it moving up and down for a few seconds until it becomes uniformly dark.
6. Rinse in cold water.

   At this point the artistry of the individual comes in; that is, the rubbing and high lighting so that work will look its best.
7. Dip the wet fingers in whiting and remove part of the sulphidizing by gentle rubbing.
8. Rinse in hot water and dry.

If unsuccessful in producing the desired effect the first time, do the whole thing over and try it again.

Silver can be cleaned quickly by giving it a cyanide dip.

Potassium cyanide.............................. ¼ pound
Water.. ½ gallon

A poor grade of cyanide (cyanide balls) is good enough, and a hot solution works instantly.

GLOSSARY

ABRASIVE. A substance used for grinding and polishing, such as emery, pumice, rotten stone, and rouge.

ANNEALING. The process of heating, with subsequent cooling, so as to soften metal and render it workable.

ANODE. The plate of metal in a plating solution by which the current enters the solution and from which metal dissolves.

AQUA REGIA. A mixture of nitric and hydrochloric acid used for dissolving gold.

ASSEMBLE. To fit and join together various parts to make a whole.

BASE METAL. Metal which combines directly with oxygen gas is termed a "base" metal.

BASTARD FILE. A coarse file for rough work.

BEADING. A border or an edge; for example, around the edge of a plate.

BEZEL. The collar or metal ring that holds a stone.

BINDING WIRE. Soft iron wire used for binding pieces of work together while soldering.

BISMUTH. A metal useful as an alloy to harden and lower the melting temperature.

BORAX SLATE. A slab of slate on which borax and water are rubbed to form a flux for soldering.

BRASS. An alloy of copper and zinc, 65 per cent copper and 35 per cent zinc.

BREAKING DOWN. Taking off the edge from a new wire scratch brush by running it against an old file.

BRITANNIA METAL. A trade name used for a good quality of pewter: 92 per cent tin, 6 per cent antimony, and 2 per cent copper.

BRONZE. An alloy of copper and tin with other metals occasionally added in small proportions.

BURNISHING. Giving a metal a very high luster by rubbing it with a smooth steel, agate, or bloodstone tool called a "burnisher."

CABOCHON. A term used to describe the shape of a stone. A smooth curved stone, no facets.

CARBON TOOL STEEL. An alloy steel that may be hardened, tempered, and annealed.

CHASING. The process of tooling the surface of metals by means of punches and a hammer.

CHASING TOOLS. Steel punches with various shaped ends. Indispensable tools for a chaser.

CONTOUR. The outline of a mass; a profile.

COTTER PIN. A piece of half-round wire bent to the shape of a U, used by craftworkers to clamp parts together for soldering.

COUNTERSINK. To bevel or make a bed on the edge of a hole.

CROCUS. An iron oxide, also known as rouge, used for polishing.

CRUCIBLE. A vessel of fire clay or graphite used for melting metals.

DAPPING DIE. A steel block with concave depressions, semispherical in shape and graduated in sizes.

DEVELOPMENT. A term used in mechanical drawing, meaning to lay out or unfold; for example, a cylinder or cone spread out in the flat.

DIVIDERS. A steel tool resembling a pair of compasses.

DRAWPLATE. A flat piece of steel with holes in graduated sizes used to reduce the size of wire.

DUCTILE. Referring to metals that can be drawn out.

ESCUTCHEON PIN. A nail with a half-round head often used as a rivet by clipping the stem.

EXTRUDED METAL. Metal that has been pushed by force through a die, much like a sausage machine.

FILLET. In patternmaking, a fillet is the concave junction formed where two surfaces meet; a very important part of any pattern.

FINE SILVER. Pure silver, free of alloy.

FLUTING. The process of making channels or grooves in the surface of the metal, as in a column.

FLUX. A substance applied to the surface of metal where soldering is to be done, to prevent oxidation of the metal.

GAUGE. The thickness of metal by number or decimal.

GERMAN SILVER. Also called nickel silver. An alloyed metal of copper, nickel, and zinc, used mostly for tableware and plated goods. Sudden changes of temperature will crack it.

GRAVERS. Tools for cutting metal, as engraving.

GRINDING. Using coarse emery on wheels to prepare a surface for finer grades.

HARD SOLDER. An alloy of silver, copper, and zinc. It always takes a red heat to melt the solder. It is used on all fine work.

HIGH LIGHTS. The elevated portions of a figured surface.

INTAGLIO. A figure or ornament cut or engraved into a substance. The reverse of a cameo.

LACQUER. A sealing wax or varnish substance, brushed or sprayed over metal to prevent tarnishing.

LIVER OF SULPHUR. A sulphur compound used for oxidizing metal.

MALLEABLE. Metal that can be extended or shaped by beating with a hammer or rolled by pressure.

MANDREL. In metal work, a tapered piece of steel, such as a ring mandrel.

MAT SURFACE. A dull finish without luster.

MATTING. The process of roughening a surface by means of punch impressions or hammer marks.

MILD STEEL. A very malleable alloy steel, easily worked, forged, and welded.

MOLDING SAND. Fine sand with a small per cent of clay. Sand in which castings are made.

PARALLEL PLIERS OR VISE. A holding tool where the jaws open and close in a parallel position at all times. Used for a better and stronger grip on the work.

PATINA. A film formed on metal by exposure and age.

PEEN OF A HAMMER. The round or wedge-shaped end of a hammer opposite the face.

PICKLE. A mixture of acids and water for cleaning metals.

PITCH. A preparation for supporting metal while it is being chased.

PLANISH. To produce a texture on a metal surface by light blows from a hammer having a polished face.

PUMICE. A volcanic lava or glass used as an abrasive for smoothing and polishing. It is used in either rock or powdered form.

PUNCH. A piece of a metal rod where one end is shaped to make individual impressions, such as center punch, chasing tools, or a drift.

RAISING. The process of fashioning a piece of metal into shape by hammering and the use of various stakes.

RAWHIDE MALLET. A useful mallet for metal workers. It is softer than wood.

REAMER. A tool used for enlarging drilled holes.

REPOUSSÉ. Ornamental metalwork formed in relief from sheet metal.

SCORING. The process of incising a line on the metal for making a sharp bend.

SNARLING IRON. A steel rod having the ends bent at right angles opposite to each other; used for raising patterns on hollow vessels. One end of the iron is fastened in the vise, the other inserted in the vessel. By striking the rod with a hammer near the vise, vibrations will raise the metal

SOFT SOLDER. An alloy of tin and lead and sometimes bismuth and cadmium. It melts at a heat lower than red heat.

STAKES. Irons of various shapes and sizes used for the shaping, forming, and planishing of metals.

STERLING SILVER. An alloyed metal, 92½ per cent fine silver and 7½ per cent copper (0.925 silver, 0.075 copper).

TAPPING. The process of cutting a thread in a hole for the purpose of receiving a screw.

TEMPLATE OR TEMPLET. A thin metal plate or cardboard cut to a special outline.

TRIPOLI. A fine earth; silica; a splendid metal polishing compound.

VERDIGRIS. A term applied to the green or bluish color on such metals as copper and brass.

WELD. To unite two pieces of metal by fusing.

INDEX

Metal, finishes on, 189–198
Mold, plaster of Paris, 36
Mushroom stake, 12

N

Napkin clips, 64
Nitric acid, 48, 92

P

Paris Exposition of Modern Arts and
    Crafts, 118, 120, 128, 134
Pattern, split, 34, 36
Patternmaking, 34
Pewter, 22, 54–58, 62, 68–74, 78,
    84–100, 104–112, 116, 120–124,
    136, 140, 146–150, 160, 162
  etching solution for, 48
  luster, 192
  plaster of Paris mold for, 36
  softening, 6
  soldering, 30
  welding, 30
Pickling, 10–14, 32, 58, 72, 74, 84, 98,
    128, 142, 144, 146, 152, 190, 192
  definition, 197
  procedure, 8
  solution, 8
Pickup tongs, 8, 9
Pictorial etching, 48
Pitch, 40–42, 197, 198
Pitch bowl, 46, 136
Pitcher, 74
Planishing, 10, 16, 38, 44, 46, 54–58,
    62–68, 72, 74, 84–100, 104, 110–
    116, 120–130, 144–158
  definition, 197
  procedure, 16
Planishing hammer, mirror finish, 3,
    10, 74, 130, 148
Plaster of Paris, 34, 36, 40, 84, 120,
    160
Platters, 70, 106
Pliers, 6, 7
Porringer, 56
Potassium sulphide (liver of sulphur),
    190–192
Pumice powder, 48, 52, 54, 70, 92, 96,
    108, 110, 114, 116, 122, 140, 148,
    158, 190, 191, 197

Punch or soup ladle, 156
Punches (chasing tools), 38, 44, 104,
    132, 197

R

Raising, 14, 15, 104, 134, 138, 162, 197
Raising hammer, 3, 14
Raising stake, 14
Rawhide mallet, 20, 94, 100, 104, 144,
    148, 158, 197
Reading lamp, 154
Repoussé work, 44, 197
Riveting, 60, 66, 76, 80, 82, 102, 116,
    126, 134, 146, 156
Rods, candlestick, 60
Roman lamp lighter, 162
Rouge cloth, 16, 54

S

Sal ammoniac, 26
Saw, 4, 60, 90, 132, 160
    (See also Jeweler's saw)
Scratch awl, 102, 104, 118, 140
Scratch brush, 191, 192
Serving trays, 100, 114, 158
Shafting, 54
Shallow hollowing, 10, 11
Shallow raising with wedge mallet, 12,
    13
Shears, 4, 10, 76
Sheet-metalworker's brake, 18, 76
Silent butler, 126
Silver, 56, 62, 64, 68, 72, 74, 78, 84–
    100, 110, 120, 124, 128, 130, 146,
    150, 156, 162, 198
  butler finish, 192
  oxidized finish, 192, 193
  sterling, 8, 197
Silver solder, 32, 72, 74, 84
Snarling iron, 46, 107
Soft cold-rolled copper or brass, 70
Soft soldering, 28, 64, 112, 197
Solder, 56, 62, 68, 74, 76, 82, 92, 96,
    100–124, 128, 130, 134, 136, 140,
    142, 152, 162
  cold, 64, 158
  dealers in, 198
  hard, 22, 146, 150
  soft, 28, 64, 118, 142, 150, 190

A CATALOGUE OF SELECTED DOVER BOOKS
IN ALL FIELDS OF INTEREST

A CATALOGUE OF SELECTED DOVER BOOKS
IN ALL FIELDS OF INTEREST

AMERICA'S OLD MASTERS, James T. Flexner. Four men emerged unexpectedly from provincial 18th century America to leadership in European art: Benjamin West, J. S. Copley, C. R. Peale, Gilbert Stuart. Brilliant coverage of lives and contributions. Revised, 1967 edition. 69 plates. 365pp. of text.

21806-6 Paperbound $3.00

FIRST FLOWERS OF OUR WILDERNESS: AMERICAN PAINTING, THE COLONIAL PERIOD, James T. Flexner. Painters, and regional painting traditions from earliest Colonial times up to the emergence of Copley, West and Peale Sr., Foster, Gustavus Hesselius, Feke, John Smibert and many anonymous painters in the primitive manner. Engaging presentation, with 162 illustrations. xxii + 368pp.

22180-6 Paperbound $3.50

THE LIGHT OF DISTANT SKIES: AMERICAN PAINTING, 1760-1835, James T. Flexner. The great generation of early American painters goes to Europe to learn and to teach: West, Copley, Gilbert Stuart and others. Allston, Trumbull, Morse; also contemporary American painters—primitives, derivatives, academics—who remained in America. 102 illustrations. xiii + 306pp. 22179-2 Paperbound $3.00

A HISTORY OF THE RISE AND PROGRESS OF THE ARTS OF DESIGN IN THE UNITED STATES, William Dunlap. Much the richest mine of information on early American painters, sculptors, architects, engravers, miniaturists, etc. The only source of information for scores of artists, the major primary source for many others. Unabridged reprint of rare original 1834 edition, with new introduction by James T. Flexner, and 394 new illustrations. Edited by Rita Weiss. 6⅝ x 9⅝.

21695-0, 21696-9, 21697-7 Three volumes, Paperbound $13.50

EPOCHS OF CHINESE AND JAPANESE ART, Ernest F. Fenollosa. From primitive Chinese art to the 20th century, thorough history, explanation of every important art period and form, including Japanese woodcuts; main stress on China and Japan, but Tibet, Korea also included. Still unexcelled for its detailed, rich coverage of cultural background, aesthetic elements, diffusion studies, particularly of the historical period. 2nd, 1913 edition. 242 illustrations. lii + 439pp. of text.

20364-6, 20365-4 Two volumes, Paperbound $6.00

THE GENTLE ART OF MAKING ENEMIES, James A. M. Whistler. Greatest wit of his day deflates Oscar Wilde, Ruskin, Swinburne; strikes back at inane critics, exhibitions, art journalism; aesthetics of impressionist revolution in most striking form. Highly readable classic by great painter. Reproduction of edition designed by Whistler. Introduction by Alfred Werner. xxxvi + 334pp.

21875-9 Paperbound $2.50

VISUAL ILLUSIONS: THEIR CAUSES, CHARACTERISTICS, AND APPLICATIONS, Matthew Luckiesh. Thorough description and discussion of optical illusion, geometric and perspective, particularly; size and shape distortions, illusions of color, of motion; natural illusions; use of illusion in art and magic, industry, etc. Most useful today with op art, also for classical art. Scores of effects illustrated. Introduction by William H. Ittleson. 100 illustrations. xxi + 252pp.

21530-X Paperbound $2.00

A HANDBOOK OF ANATOMY FOR ART STUDENTS, Arthur Thomson. Thorough, virtually exhaustive coverage of skeletal structure, musculature, etc. Full text, supplemented by anatomical diagrams and drawings and by photographs of undraped figures. Unique in its comparison of male and female forms, pointing out differences of contour, texture, form. 211 figures, 40 drawings, 86 photographs. xx + 459pp. 5⅜ x 8⅜.

21163-0 Paperbound $3.50

150 MASTERPIECES OF DRAWING, Selected by Anthony Toney. Full page reproductions of drawings from the early 16th to the end of the 18th century, all beautifully reproduced: Rembrandt, Michelangelo, Dürer, Fragonard, Urs, Graf, Wouwerman, many others. First-rate browsing book, model book for artists. xviii + 150pp. 8⅜ x 11¼.

21032-4 Paperbound $2.50

THE LATER WORK OF AUBREY BEARDSLEY, Aubrey Beardsley. Exotic, erotic, ironic masterpieces in full maturity: Comedy Ballet, Venus and Tannhauser, Pierrot, Lysistrata, Rape of the Lock, Savoy material, Ali Baba, Volpone, etc. This material revolutionized the art world, and is still powerful, fresh, brilliant. With The Early Work, all Beardsley's finest work. 174 plates, 2 in color. xiv + 176pp. 8⅛ x 11.

21817-1 Paperbound $3.00

DRAWINGS OF REMBRANDT, Rembrandt van Rijn. Complete reproduction of fabulously rare edition by Lippmann and Hofstede de Groot, completely reedited, updated, improved by Prof. Seymour Slive, Fogg Museum. Portraits, Biblical sketches, landscapes, Oriental types, nudes, episodes from classical mythology—All Rembrandt's fertile genius. Also selection of drawings by his pupils and followers. "Stunning volumes," Saturday Review. 550 illustrations. lxxviii + 552pp. 9⅛ x 12¼.

21485-0, 21486-9 Two volumes, Paperbound $7.00

THE DISASTERS OF WAR, Francisco Goya. One of the masterpieces of Western civilization—83 etchings that record Goya's shattering, bitter reaction to the Napoleonic war that swept through Spain after the insurrection of 1808 and to war in general. Reprint of the first edition, with three additional plates from Boston's Museum of Fine Arts. All plates facsimile size. Introduction by Philip Hofer, Fogg Museum. v + 97pp. 9⅜ x 8¼.

21872-4 Paperbound $2.00

GRAPHIC WORKS OF ODILON REDON. Largest collection of Redon's graphic works ever assembled: 172 lithographs, 28 etchings and engravings, 9 drawings. These include some of his most famous works. All the plates from Odilon Redon: oeuvre graphique complet, plus additional plates. New introduction and caption translations by Alfred Werner. 209 illustrations. xxvii + 209pp. 9⅛ x 12¼.

21966-8 Paperbound $4.00

DESIGN BY ACCIDENT; A BOOK OF "ACCIDENTAL EFFECTS" FOR ARTISTS AND DESIGNERS, James F. O'Brien. Create your own unique, striking, imaginative effects by "controlled accident" interaction of materials: paints and lacquers, oil and water based paints, splatter, crackling materials, shatter, similar items. Everything you do will be different; first book on this limitless art, so useful to both fine artist and commercial artist. Full instructions. 192 plates showing "accidents," 8 in color. viii + 215pp. 8⅜ x 11¼. 21942-9 Paperbound $3.50

THE BOOK OF SIGNS, Rudolf Koch. Famed German type designer draws 493 beautiful symbols: religious, mystical, alchemical, imperial, property marks, runes, etc. Remarkable fusion of traditional and modern. Good for suggestions of timelessness, smartness, modernity. Text. vi + 104pp. 6⅛ x 9¼. 20162-7 Paperbound $1.25

HISTORY OF INDIAN AND INDONESIAN ART, Ananda K. Coomaraswamy. An unabridged republication of one of the finest books by a great scholar in Eastern art. Rich in descriptive material, history, social backgrounds; Sunga reliefs, Rajput paintings, Gupta temples, Burmese frescoes, textiles, jewelry, sculpture, etc. 400 photos. viii + 423pp. 6⅜ x 9¾. 21436-2 Paperbound $4.00

PRIMITIVE ART, Franz Boas. America's foremost anthropologist surveys textiles, ceramics, woodcarving, basketry, metalwork, etc.; patterns, technology, creation of symbols, style origins. All areas of world, but very full on Northwest Coast Indians. More than 350 illustrations of baskets, boxes, totem poles, weapons, etc. 378 pp. 20025-6 Paperbound $3.00

THE GENTLEMAN AND CABINET MAKER'S DIRECTOR, Thomas Chippendale. Full reprint (third edition, 1762) of most influential furniture book of all time, by master cabinetmaker. 200 plates, illustrating chairs, sofas, mirrors, tables, cabinets, plus 24 photographs of surviving pieces. Biographical introduction by N. Bienenstock. vi + 249pp. 9⅞ x 12¾. 21601-2 Paperbound $4.00

AMERICAN ANTIQUE FURNITURE, Edgar G. Miller, Jr. The basic coverage of all American furniture before 1840. Individual chapters cover type of furniture—clocks, tables, sideboards, etc.—chronologically, with inexhaustible wealth of data. More than 2100 photographs, all identified, commented on. Essential to all early American collectors. Introduction by H. E. Keyes. vi + 1106pp. 7⅞ x 10¾. 21599-7, 21600-4 Two volumes, Paperbound $11.00

PENNSYLVANIA DUTCH AMERICAN FOLK ART, Henry J. Kauffman. 279 photos, 28 drawings of tulipware, Fraktur script, painted tinware, toys, flowered furniture, quilts, samplers, hex signs, house interiors, etc. Full descriptive text. Excellent for tourist, rewarding for designer, collector. Map. 146pp. 7⅞ x 10¾. 21205-X Paperbound $2.50

EARLY NEW ENGLAND GRAVESTONE RUBBINGS, Edmund V. Gillon, Jr. 43 photographs, 226 carefully reproduced rubbings show heavily symbolic, sometimes macabre early gravestones, up to early 19th century. Remarkable early American primitive art, occasionally strikingly beautiful; always powerful. Text. xxvi + 207pp. 8⅜ x 11¼. 21380-3 Paperbound $3.50

ALPHABETS AND ORNAMENTS, Ernst Lehner. Well-known pictorial source for decorative alphabets, script examples, cartouches, frames, decorative title pages, calligraphic initials, borders, similar material. 14th to 19th century, mostly European. Useful in almost any graphic arts designing, varied styles. 750 illustrations. 256pp. 7 x 10.   21905-4 Paperbound $4.00

PAINTING: A CREATIVE APPROACH, Norman Colquhoun. For the beginner simple guide provides an instructive approach to painting: major stumbling blocks for beginner; overcoming them, technical points; paints and pigments; oil painting; watercolor and other media and color. New section on "plastic" paints. Glossary. Formerly *Paint Your Own Pictures*. 221pp.   22000-1 Paperbound $1.75

THE ENJOYMENT AND USE OF COLOR, Walter Sargent. Explanation of the relations between colors themselves and between colors in nature and art, including hundreds of little-known facts about color values, intensities, effects of high and low illumination, complementary colors. Many practical hints for painters, references to great masters. 7 color plates, 29 illustrations. x + 274pp.
20944-X Paperbound $2.75

THE NOTEBOOKS OF LEONARDO DA VINCI, compiled and edited by Jean Paul Richter. 1566 extracts from original manuscripts reveal the full range of Leonardo's versatile genius: all his writings on painting, sculpture, architecture, anatomy, astronomy, geography, topography, physiology, mining, music, etc., in both Italian and English, with 186 plates of manuscript pages and more than 500 additional drawings. Includes studies for the Last Supper, the lost Sforza monument, and other works. Total of xlvii + 866pp 7⅞ x 10¾
22572-0, 22573-9 Two volumes, Paperbound $10.00

MONTGOMERY WARD CATALOGUE OF 1895. Tea gowns, yards of flannel and pillow-case lace, stereoscopes, books of gospel hymns, the New Improved Singer Sewing Machine, side saddles, milk skimmers, straight-edged razors, high-button shoes, spittoons, and on and on . . . listing some 25,000 items, practically all illustrated. Essential to the shoppers of the 1890's, it is our truest record of the period. Unaltered reprint of Issue No. 57, Spring and Summer 1895. Introduction by Boris Emmet. Innumerable illustrations. xiii + 624pp. 8½ x 11⅝.
22377-9 Paperbound $6.95

THE CRYSTAL PALACE EXHIBITION ILLUSTRATED CATALOGUE (LONDON, 1851). One of the wonders of the modern world—the Crystal Palace Exhibition in which all the nations of the civilized world exhibited their achievements in the arts and sciences—presented in an equally important illustrated catalogue. More than 1700 items pictured with accompanying text—ceramics, textiles, cast-iron work, carpets, pianos, sleds, razors, wall-papers, billiard tables, beehives, silverware and hundreds of other artifacts—represent the focal point of Victorian culture in the Western World. Probably the largest collection of Victorian decorative art ever assembled—indispensable for antiquarians and designers. Unabridged republication of the Art Journal Catalogue of the Great Exhibition of 1851, with all terminal essays. New introduction by John Gloag, F.S.A. xxxiv + 426pp. 9 x 12.
22503-8 Paperbound $4.50

A History of Costume, Carl Köhler. Definitive history, based on surviving pieces of clothing primarily, and paintings, statues, etc. secondarily. Highly readable text, supplemented by 594 illustrations of costumes of the ancient Mediterranean peoples, Greece and Rome, the Teutonic prehistoric period; costumes of the Middle Ages, Renaissance, Baroque, 18th and 19th centuries. Clear, measured patterns are provided for many clothing articles. Approach is practical throughout. Enlarged by Emma von Sichart. 464pp.   21030-8 Paperbound $3.50

Oriental Rugs, Antique and Modern, Walter A. Hawley. A complete and authoritative treatise on the Oriental rug—where they are made, by whom and how, designs and symbols, characteristics in detail of the six major groups, how to distinguish them and how to buy them. Detailed technical data is provided on periods, weaves, warps, wefts, textures, sides, ends and knots, although no technical background is required for an understanding. 11 color plates, 80 halftones, 4 maps. vi + 320pp. 6⅛ x 9⅛.   22366-3 Paperbound $5.00

Ten Books on Architecture, Vitruvius. By any standards the most important book on architecture ever written. Early Roman discussion of aesthetics of building, construction methods, orders, sites, and every other aspect of architecture has inspired, instructed architecture for about 2,000 years. Stands behind Palladio, Michelangelo, Bramante, Wren, countless others. Definitive Morris H. Morgan translation. 68 illustrations. xii + 331pp.   20645-9 Paperbound $2.50

The Four Books of Architecture, Andrea Palladio. Translated into every major Western European language in the two centuries following its publication in 1570, this has been one of the most influential books in the history of architecture. Complete reprint of the 1738 Isaac Ware edition. New introduction by Adolf Placzek, Columbia Univ. 216 plates. xxii + 110pp. of text. 9½ x 12¾.
21308-0 Clothbound $10.00

Sticks and Stones: A Study of American Architecture and Civilization, Lewis Mumford.One of the great classics of American cultural history. American architecture from the medieval-inspired earliest forms to the early 20th century; evolution of structure and style, and reciprocal influences on environment. 21 photographic illustrations. 238pp.   20202-X Paperbound $2.00

The American Builder's Companion, Asher Benjamin. The most widely used early 19th century architectural style and source book, for colonial up into Greek Revival periods. Extensive development of geometry of carpentering, construction of sashes, frames, doors, stairs; plans and elevations of domestic and other buildings. Hundreds of thousands of houses were built according to this book, now invaluable to historians, architects, restorers, etc. 1827 edition. 59 plates. 114pp. 7⅞ x 10¾.
22236-5 Paperbound $3.00

Dutch Houses in the Hudson Valley Before 1776, Helen Wilkinson Reynolds. The standard survey of the Dutch colonial house and outbuildings, with constructional features, decoration, and local history associated with individual homesteads. Introduction by Franklin D. Roosevelt. Map. 150 illustrations. 469pp. 6⅝ x 9¼.   21469-9 Paperbound $4.00

THE ARCHITECTURE OF COUNTRY HOUSES, Andrew J. Downing. Together with Vaux's *Villas and Cottages* this is the basic book for Hudson River Gothic architecture of the middle Victorian period. Full, sound discussions of general aspects of housing, architecture, style, decoration, furnishing, together with scores of detailed house plans, illustrations of specific buildings, accompanied by full text. Perhaps the most influential single American architectural book. 1850 edition. Introduction by J. Stewart Johnson. 321 figures, 34 architectural designs. xvi + 560pp.
22003-6 Paperbound $4.00

LOST EXAMPLES OF COLONIAL ARCHITECTURE, John Mead Howells. Full-page photographs of buildings that have disappeared or been so altered as to be denatured, including many designed by major early American architects. 245 plates. xvii + 248pp. 7⅞ x 10¾. 21143-6 Paperbound $3.50

DOMESTIC ARCHITECTURE OF THE AMERICAN COLONIES AND OF THE EARLY REPUBLIC, Fiske Kimball. Foremost architect and restorer of Williamsburg and Monticello covers nearly 200 homes between 1620-1825. Architectural details, construction, style features, special fixtures, floor plans, etc. Generally considered finest work in its area. 219 illustrations of houses, doorways, windows, capital mantels. xx + 314pp. 7⅞ x 10¾. 21743-4 Paperbound $4.00

EARLY AMERICAN ROOMS: 1650-1858, edited by Russell Hawes Kettell. Tour of 12 rooms, each representative of a different era in American history and each furnished, decorated, designed and occupied in the style of the era. 72 plans and elevations, 8-page color section, etc., show fabrics, wall papers, arrangements, etc. Full descriptive text. xvii + 200pp. of text. 8⅜ x 11¼.
21633-0 Paperbound $5.00

THE FITZWILLIAM VIRGINAL BOOK, edited by J. Fuller Maitland and W. B. Squire. Full modern printing of famous early 17th-century ms. volume of 300 works by Morley, Byrd, Bull, Gibbons, etc. For piano or other modern keyboard instrument; easy to read format. xxxvi + 938pp. 8⅜ x 11.
21068-5, 21069-3 Two volumes, Paperbound $10.00

KEYBOARD MUSIC, Johann Sebastian Bach. Bach Gesellschaft edition. A rich selection of Bach's masterpieces for the harpsichord: the six English Suites, six French Suites, the six Partitas (Clavierübung part I), the Goldberg Variations (Clavierübung part IV), the fifteen Two-Part Inventions and the fifteen Three-Part Sinfonias. Clearly reproduced on large sheets with ample margins, eminently playable. vi + 312pp. 8⅛ x 11. 22360-4 Paperbound $5.00

THE MUSIC OF BACH: AN INTRODUCTION, Charles Sanford Terry. A fine, non-technical introduction to Bach's music, both instrumental and vocal. Covers organ music, chamber music, passion music, other types. Analyzes themes, developments, innovations. x + 114pp. 21075-8 Paperbound $1.25

BEETHOVEN AND HIS NINE SYMPHONIES, Sir George Grove. Noted British musicologist provides best history, analysis, commentary on symphonies. Very thorough, rigorously accurate; necessary to both advanced student and amateur music lover. 436 musical passages. vii + 407 pp. 20334-4 Paperbound $2.75

JOHANN SEBASTIAN BACH, Philipp Spitta. One of the great classics of musicology, this definitive analysis of Bach's music (and life) has never been surpassed. Lucid, nontechnical analyses of hundreds of pieces (30 pages devoted to St. Matthew Passion, 26 to B Minor Mass). Also includes major analysis of 18th-century music. 450 musical examples. 40-page musical supplement. Total of xx + 1799pp.
(EUK) 22278-0, 22279-9 Two volumes, Clothbound $17.50

MOZART AND HIS PIANO CONCERTOS, Cuthbert Girdlestone. The only full-length study of an important area of Mozart's creativity. Provides detailed analyses of all 23 concertos, traces inspirational sources. 417 musical examples. Second edition. 509pp.
(USO) 21271-8 Paperbound $3.50

THE PERFECT WAGNERITE: A COMMENTARY ON THE NIBLUNG'S RING, George Bernard Shaw. Brilliant and still relevant criticism in remarkable essays on Wagner's Ring cycle, Shaw's ideas on political and social ideology behind the plots, role of Leitmotifs, vocal requisites, etc. Prefaces. xxi + 136pp.
21707-8 Paperbound $1.50

DON GIOVANNI, W. A. Mozart. Complete libretto, modern English translation; biographies of composer and librettist; accounts of early performances and critical reaction. Lavishly illustrated. All the material you need to understand and appreciate this great work. Dover Opera Guide and Libretto Series; translated and introduced by Ellen Bleiler. 92 illustrations. 209pp.
21134-7 Paperbound $1.50

HIGH FIDELITY SYSTEMS: A LAYMAN'S GUIDE, Roy F. Allison. All the basic information you need for setting up your own audio system: high fidelity and stereo record players, tape records, F.M. Connections, adjusting tone arm, cartridge, checking needle alignment, positioning speakers, phasing speakers, adjusting hums, trouble-shooting, maintenance, and similar topics. Enlarged 1965 edition. More than 50 charts, diagrams, photos. iv + 91pp.
21514-8 Paperbound $1.25

REPRODUCTION OF SOUND, Edgar Villchur. Thorough coverage for laymen of high fidelity systems, reproducing systems in general, needles, amplifiers, preamps, loudspeakers, feedback, explaining physical background. "A rare talent for making technicalities vividly comprehensible," R. Darrell, High Fidelity. 69 figures. iv + 92pp.
21515-6 Paperbound $1.25

HEAR ME TALKIN' TO YA: THE STORY OF JAZZ AS TOLD BY THE MEN WHO MADE IT, Nat Shapiro and Nat Hentoff. Louis Armstrong, Fats Waller, Jo Jones, Clarence Williams, Billy Holiday, Duke Ellington, Jelly Roll Morton and dozens of other jazz greats tell how it was in Chicago's South Side, New Orleans, depression Harlem and the modern West Coast as jazz was born and grew. xvi + 429pp.
21726-4 Paperbound $2.50

FABLES OF AESOP, translated by Sir Roger L'Estrange. A reproduction of the very rare 1931 Paris edition; a selection of the most interesting fables, together with 50 imaginative drawings by Alexander Calder. v + 128pp. 6½x9¼.
21780-9 Paperbound $1.50

AGAINST THE GRAIN (A REBOURS), Joris K. Huysmans. Filled with weird images, evidences of a bizarre imagination, exotic experiments with hallucinatory drugs, rich tastes and smells and the diversions of its sybarite hero Duc Jean des Esseintes, this classic novel pushed 19th-century literary decadence to its limits. Full un-abridged edition. Do not confuse this with abridged editions generally sold. Intro-duction by Havelock Ellis. xlix + 206pp. 22190-3 Paperbound $2.00

VARIORUM SHAKESPEARE: HAMLET. Edited by Horace H. Furness; a landmark of American scholarship. Exhaustive footnotes and appendices treat all doubtful words and phrases, as well as suggested critical emendations throughout the play's history. First volume contains editor's own text, collated with all Quartos and Folios. Second volume contains full first Quarto, translations of Shakespeare's sources (Belleforest, and Saxo Grammaticus), Der Bestrafte Brudermord, and many essays on critical and historical points of interest by major authorities of past and present. Includes details of staging and costuming over the years. By far the best edition available for serious students of Shakespeare. Total of xx + 905pp.
21004-9, 21005-7, 2 volumes, Paperbound $7.00

A LIFE OF WILLIAM SHAKESPEARE, Sir Sidney Lee. This is the standard life of Shakespeare, summarizing everything known about Shakespeare and his plays. Incredibly rich in material, broad in coverage, clear and judicious, it has served thousands as the best introduction to Shakespeare. 1931 edition. 9 plates. xxix + 792pp. (USO) 21967-4 Paperbound $3.75

MASTERS OF THE DRAMA, John Gassner. Most comprehensive history of the drama in print, covering every tradition from Greeks to modern Europe and America, including India, Far East, etc. Covers more than 800 dramatists, 2000 plays, with biographical material, plot summaries, theatre history, criticism, etc. "Best of its kind in English," New Republic. 77 illustrations. xxii + 890pp.
20100-7 Clothbound $8.50

THE EVOLUTION OF THE ENGLISH LANGUAGE, George McKnight. The growth of English, from the 14th century to the present. Unusual, non-technical account presents basic information in very interesting form: sound shifts, change in grammar and syntax, vocabulary growth, similar topics. Abundantly illustrated with quota-tions. Formerly Modern English in the Making. xii + 590pp.
21932-1 Paperbound $3.50

AN ETYMOLOGICAL DICTIONARY OF MODERN ENGLISH, Ernest Weekley. Fullest, richest work of its sort, by foremost British lexicographer. Detailed word histories, including many colloquial and archaic words; extensive quotations. Do not con-fuse this with the Concise Etymological Dictionary, which is much abridged. Total of xxvii + 830pp. 6½ x 9¼.
21873-2, 21874-0 Two volumes, Paperbound $6.00

FLATLAND: A ROMANCE OF MANY DIMENSIONS, E. A. Abbott. Classic of science-fiction explores ramifications of life in a two-dimensional world, and what happens when a three-dimensional being intrudes. Amusing reading, but also use-ful as introduction to thought about hyperspace. Introduction by Banesh Hoffmann. 16 illustrations. xx + 103pp. 20001-9 Paperbound $1.00

POEMS OF ANNE BRADSTREET, edited with an introduction by Robert Hutchinson. A new selection of poems by America's first poet and perhaps the first significant woman poet in the English language. 48 poems display her development in works of considerable variety—love poems, domestic poems, religious meditations, formal elegies, "quaternions," etc. Notes, bibliography. viii + 222pp.
22160-1 Paperbound $2.00

THREE GOTHIC NOVELS: THE CASTLE OF OTRANTO BY HORACE WALPOLE; VATHEK BY WILLIAM BECKFORD; THE VAMPYRE BY JOHN POLIDORI, WITH FRAGMENT OF A NOVEL BY LORD BYRON, edited by E. F. Bleiler. The first Gothic novel, by Walpole; the finest Oriental tale in English, by Beckford; powerful Romantic supernatural story in versions by Polidori and Byron. All extremely important in history of literature; all still exciting, packed with supernatural thrills, ghosts, haunted castles, magic, etc. xl + 291pp.
21232-7 Paperbound $2.00

THE BEST TALES OF HOFFMANN, E. T. A. Hoffmann. 10 of Hoffmann's most important stories, in modern re-editings of standard translations: Nutcracker and the King of Mice, Signor Formica, Automata, The Sandman, Rath Krespel, The Golden Flowerpot, Master Martin the Cooper, The Mines of Falun, The King's Betrothed, A New Year's Eve Adventure. 7 illustrations by Hoffmann. Edited by E. F. Bleiler. xxxix + 419pp.
21793-0 Paperbound $2.50

GHOST AND HORROR STORIES OF AMBROSE BIERCE, Ambrose Bierce. 23 strikingly modern stories of the horrors latent in the human mind: The Eyes of the Panther, The Damned Thing, An Occurrence at Owl Creek Bridge, An Inhabitant of Carcosa, etc., plus the dream-essay, Visions of the Night. Edited by E. F. Bleiler. xxii + 199pp.
20767-6 Paperbound $1.50

BEST GHOST STORIES OF J. S. LEFANU, J. Sheridan LeFanu. Finest stories by Victorian master often considered greatest supernatural writer of all. Carmilla, Green Tea, The Haunted Baronet, The Familiar, and 12 others. Most never before available in the U. S. A. Edited by E. F. Bleiler. 8 illustrations from Victorian publications. xvii + 467pp.
20415-4 Paperbound $3.00

THE TIME STREAM, THE GREATEST ADVENTURE, AND THE PURPLE SAPPHIRE— THREE SCIENCE FICTION NOVELS, John Taine (Eric Temple Bell). Great American mathematician was also foremost science fiction novelist of the 1920's. *The Time Stream,* one of all-time classics, uses concepts of circular time; *The Greatest Adventure,* incredibly ancient biological experiments from Antarctica threaten to escape; The *Purple Sapphire,* superscience, lost races in Central Tibet, survivors of the Great Race. 4 illustrations by Frank R. Paul. v + 532pp.
21180-0 Paperbound $3.00

SEVEN SCIENCE FICTION NOVELS, H. G. Wells. The standard collection of the great novels. Complete, unabridged. *First Men in the Moon, Island of Dr. Moreau, War of the Worlds, Food of the Gods, Invisible Man, Time Machine, In the Days of the Comet.* Not only science fiction fans, but every educated person owes it to himself to read these novels. 1015pp.
20264-X Clothbound $5.00

LAST AND FIRST MEN AND STAR MAKER, TWO SCIENCE FICTION NOVELS, Olaf Stapledon. Greatest future histories in science fiction. In the first, human intelligence is the "hero," through strange paths of evolution, interplanetary invasions, incredible technologies, near extinctions and reemergences. Star Maker describes the quest of a band of star rovers for intelligence itself, through time and space; weird inhuman civilizations, crustacean minds, symbiotic worlds, etc. Complete, unabridged. v + 438pp. 21962-3 Paperbound $2.50

THREE PROPHETIC NOVELS, H. G. WELLS. Stages of a consistently planned future for mankind. *When the Sleeper Wakes,* and *A Story of the Days to Come,* anticipate *Brave New World* and *1984,* in the 21st Century; *The Time Machine,* only complete version in print, shows farther future and the end of mankind. All show Wells's greatest gifts as storyteller and novelist. Edited by E. F. Bleiler. x + 335pp. (USO) 20605-X Paperbound $2.25

THE DEVIL'S DICTIONARY, Ambrose Bierce. America's own Oscar Wilde— Ambrose Bierce—offers his barbed iconoclastic wisdom in over 1,000 definitions hailed by H. L. Mencken as "some of the most gorgeous witticisms in the English language." 145pp. 20487-1 Paperbound $1.25

MAX AND MORITZ, Wilhelm Busch. Great children's classic, father of comic strip, of two bad boys, Max and Moritz. Also Ker and Plunk (Plisch und Plumm), Cat and Mouse, Deceitful Henry, Ice-Peter, The Boy and the Pipe, and five other pieces. Original German, with English translation. Edited by H. Arthur Klein; translations by various hands and H. Arthur Klein. vi + 216pp.
20181-3 Paperbound $2.00

PIGS IS PIGS AND OTHER FAVORITES, Ellis Parker Butler. The title story is one of the best humor short stories, as Mike Flannery obfuscates biology and English. Also included, That Pup of Murchison's, The Great American Pie Company, and Perkins of Portland. 14 illustrations. v + 109pp. 21532-6 Paperbound $1.00

THE PETERKIN PAPERS, Lucretia P. Hale. It takes genius to be as stupidly mad as the Peterkins, as they decide to become wise, celebrate the "Fourth," keep a cow, and otherwise strain the resources of the Lady from Philadelphia. Basic book of American humor. 153 illustrations. 219pp. 20794-3 Paperbound $1.50

PERRAULT'S FAIRY TALES, translated by A. E. Johnson and S. R. Littlewood, with 34 full-page illustrations by Gustave Doré. All the original Perrault stories— Cinderella, Sleeping Beauty, Bluebeard, Little Red Riding Hood, Puss in Boots, Tom Thumb, etc.—with their witty verse morals and the magnificent illustrations of Doré. One of the five or six great books of European fairy tales. viii + 117pp. 8⅛ x 11. 22311-6 Paperbound $2.00

OLD HUNGARIAN FAIRY TALES, Baroness Orczy. Favorites translated and adapted by author of the *Scarlet Pimpernel.* Eight fairy tales include "The Suitors of Princess Fire-Fly," "The Twin Hunchbacks," "Mr. Cuttlefish's Love Story," and "The Enchanted Cat." This little volume of magic and adventure will captivate children as it has for generations. 90 drawings by Montagu Barstow. 96pp.
(USO) 22293-4 Paperbound $1.95

THE RED FAIRY BOOK, Andrew Lang. Lang's color fairy books have long been children's favorites. This volume includes Rapunzel, Jack and the Bean-stalk and 35 other stories, familiar and unfamiliar. 4 plates, 93 illustrations x + 367pp.
21673-X Paperbound $2.50

THE BLUE FAIRY BOOK, Andrew Lang. Lang's tales come from all countries and all times. Here are 37 tales from Grimm, the Arabian Nights, Greek Mythology, and other fascinating sources. 8 plates, 130 illustrations. xi + 390pp.
21437-0 Paperbound $2.50

HOUSEHOLD STORIES BY THE BROTHERS GRIMM. Classic English-language edition of the well-known tales — Rumpelstiltskin, Snow White, Hansel and Gretel, The Twelve Brothers, Faithful John, Rapunzel, Tom Thumb (52 stories in all). Translated into simple, straightforward English by Lucy Crane. Ornamented with headpieces, vignettes, elaborate decorative initials and a dozen full-page illustrations by Walter Crane. x + 269pp.
21080-4 Paperbound $2.50

THE MERRY ADVENTURES OF ROBIN HOOD, Howard Pyle. The finest modern versions of the traditional ballads and tales about the great English outlaw. Howard Pyle's complete prose version, with every word, every illustration of the first edition. Do not confuse this facsimile of the original (1883) with modern editions that change text or illustrations. 23 plates plus many page decorations. xxii + 296pp.
22043-5 Paperbound $2.50

THE STORY OF KING ARTHUR AND HIS KNIGHTS, Howard Pyle. The finest children's version of the life of King Arthur; brilliantly retold by Pyle, with 48 of his most imaginative illustrations. xviii + 313pp. 6⅛ x 9¼.
21445-1 Paperbound $2.50

THE WONDERFUL WIZARD OF OZ, L. Frank Baum. America's finest children's book in facsimile of first edition with all Denslow illustrations in full color. The edition a child should have. Introduction by Martin Gardner. 23 color plates, scores of drawings. iv + 267pp.
20691-2 Paperbound $2.25

THE MARVELOUS LAND OF OZ, L. Frank Baum. The second Oz book, every bit as imaginative as the Wizard. The hero is a boy named Tip, but the Scarecrow and the Tin Woodman are back, as is the Oz magic. 16 color plates, 120 drawings by John R. Neill. 287pp.
20692-0 Paperbound $2.50

THE MAGICAL MONARCH OF MO, L. Frank Baum. Remarkable adventures in a land even stranger than Oz. The best of Baum's books not in the Oz series. 15 color plates and dozens of drawings by Frank Verbeck. xviii + 237pp.
21892-9 Paperbound $2.00

THE BAD CHILD'S BOOK OF BEASTS, MORE BEASTS FOR WORSE CHILDREN, A MORAL ALPHABET, Hilaire Belloc. Three complete humor classics in one volume. Be kind to the frog, and do not call him names . . . and 28 other whimsical animals. Familiar favorites and some not so well known. Illustrated by Basil Blackwell. 156pp.
(USO) 20749-8 Paperbound $1.25

EAST O' THE SUN AND WEST O' THE MOON, George W. Dasent. Considered the best of all translations of these Norwegian folk tales, this collection has been enjoyed by generations of children (and folklorists too). Includes True and Untrue, Why the Sea is Salt, East O' the Sun and West O' the Moon, Why the Bear is Stumpy-Tailed, Boots and the Troll, The Cock and the Hen, Rich Peter the Pedlar, and 52 more. The only edition with all 59 tales. 77 illustrations by Erik Werenskiold and Theodor Kittelsen. xv + 418pp. 22521-6 Paperbound $3.00

GOOPS AND HOW TO BE THEM, Gelett Burgess. Classic of tongue-in-cheek humor, masquerading as etiquette book. 87 verses, twice as many cartoons, show mischievous Goops as they demonstrate to children virtues of table manners, neatness, courtesy, etc. Favorite for generations. viii + 88pp. 6½ x 9¼. 22233-0 Paperbound $1.25

ALICE'S ADVENTURES UNDER GROUND, Lewis Carroll. The first version, quite different from the final *Alice in Wonderland,* printed out by Carroll himself with his own illustrations. Complete facsimile of the "million dollar" manuscript Carroll gave to Alice Liddell in 1864. Introduction by Martin Gardner. viii + 96pp. Title and dedication pages in color. 21482-6 Paperbound $1.25

THE BROWNIES, THEIR BOOK, Palmer Cox. Small as mice, cunning as foxes, exuberant and full of mischief, the Brownies go to the zoo, toy shop, seashore, circus, etc., in 24 verse adventures and 266 illustrations. Long a favorite, since their first appearance in St. Nicholas Magazine. xi + 144pp. 6⅝ x 9¼. 21265-3 Paperbound $1.75

SONGS OF CHILDHOOD, Walter De La Mare. Published (under the pseudonym Walter Ramal) when De La Mare was only 29, this charming collection has long been a favorite children's book. A facsimile of the first edition in paper, the 47 poems capture the simplicity of the nursery rhyme and the ballad, including such lyrics as I Met Eve, Tartary, The Silver Penny. vii + 106pp. 21972-0 Paperbound $1.25

THE COMPLETE NONSENSE OF EDWARD LEAR, Edward Lear. The finest 19th-century humorist-cartoonist in full: all nonsense limericks, zany alphabets, Owl and Pussycat, songs, nonsense botany, and more than 500 illustrations by Lear himself. Edited by Holbrook Jackson. xxix + 287pp (USO) 20167-8 Paperbound $2.00

BILLY WHISKERS: THE AUTOBIOGRAPHY OF A GOAT, Frances Trego Montgomery. A favorite of children since the early 20th century, here are the escapades of that rambunctious, irresistible and mischievous goat—Billy Whiskers. Much in the spirit of *Pooh's Dad Boy,* this is a book that children never tire of reading or hearing. All the original familiar illustrations by W. H. Fry are included: 6 color plates, 18 black and white drawings. 159pp. 22345-0 Paperbound $2.00

MOTHER GOOSE MELODIES, Faithful republication of the fabulously rare Munroe and Francis "copyright 1833" Boston edition—the most important Mother Goose collection, usually referred to as the "original." Familiar rhymes plus many rare ones, with wonderful old woodcut illustrations. Edited by E. F. Bleiler. 128pp. 4½ x 6⅜. 22577-1 Paperbound $1.25

Two Little Savages; Being the Adventures of Two Boys Who Lived as Indians and What They Learned, Ernest Thompson Seton. Great classic of nature and boyhood provides a vast range of woodlore in most palatable form, a genuinely entertaining story. Two farm boys build a teepee in woods and live in it for a month, working out Indian solutions to living problems, star lore, birds and animals, plants, etc. 293 illustrations. vii + 286pp.

20985-7 Paperbound $2.50

Peter Piper's Practical Principles of Plain & Perfect Pronunciation. Alliterative jingles and tongue-twisters of surprising charm, that made their first appearance in America about 1830. Republished in full with the spirited woodcut illustrations from this earliest American edition. 32pp. 4½ x 6⅜.

22560-7 Paperbound $1.00

Science Experiments and Amusements for Children, Charles Vivian. 73 easy experiments, requiring only materials found at home or easily available, such as candles, coins, steel wool, etc.; illustrate basic phenomena like vacuum, simple chemical reaction, etc. All safe. Modern, well-planned. Formerly *Science Games for Children.* 102 photos, numerous drawings. 96pp. 6⅛ x 9¼.

21856-2 Paperbound $1.25

An Introduction to Chess Moves and Tactics Simply Explained, Leonard Barden. Informal intermediate introduction, quite strong in explaining reasons for moves. Covers basic material, tactics, important openings, traps, positional play in middle game, end game. Attempts to isolate patterns and recurrent configurations. Formerly *Chess.* 58 figures. 102pp. (USO) 21210-6 Paperbound $1.25

Lasker's Manual of Chess, Dr. Emanuel Lasker. Lasker was not only one of the five great World Champions, he was also one of the ablest expositors, theorists, and analysts. In many ways, his Manual, permeated with his philosophy of battle, filled with keen insights, is one of the greatest works ever written on chess. Filled with analyzed games by the great players. A single-volume library that will profit almost any chess player, beginner or master. 308 diagrams. xli x 349pp.

20640-8 Paperbound $2.75

The Master Book of Mathematical Recreations, Fred Schuh. In opinion of many the finest work ever prepared on mathematical puzzles, stunts, recreations; exhaustively thorough explanations of mathematics involved, analysis of effects, citation of puzzles and games. Mathematics involved is elementary. Translated by F. Göbel. 194 figures. xxiv + 430pp. 22134-2 Paperbound $3.00

Mathematics, Magic and Mystery, Martin Gardner. Puzzle editor for Scientific American explains mathematics behind various mystifying tricks: card tricks, stage "mind reading," coin and match tricks, counting out games, geometric dissections, etc. Probability sets, theory of numbers clearly explained. Also provides more than 400 tricks, guaranteed to work, that you can do. 135 illustrations. xii + 176pp.

20338-2 Paperbound $1.50

MATHEMATICAL PUZZLES FOR BEGINNERS AND ENTHUSIASTS, Geoffrey Mott-Smith. 189 puzzles from easy to difficult—involving arithmetic, logic, algebra, properties of digits, probability, etc.—for enjoyment and mental stimulus. Explanation of mathematical principles behind the puzzles. 135 illustrations. viii + 248pp.
20198-8 Paperbound $1.75

PAPER FOLDING FOR BEGINNERS, William D. Murray and Francis J. Rigney. Easiest book on the market, clearest instructions on making interesting, beautiful origami. Sail boats, cups, roosters, frogs that move legs, bonbon boxes, standing birds, etc. 40 projects; more than 275 diagrams and photographs. 94pp.
20713-7 Paperbound $1.00

TRICKS AND GAMES ON THE POOL TABLE, Fred Herrmann. 79 tricks and games— some solitaires, some for two or more players, some competitive games—to entertain you between formal games. Mystifying shots and throws, unusual caroms, tricks involving such props as cork, coins, a hat, etc. Formerly *Fun on the Pool Table*. 77 figures. 95pp.
21814-7 Paperbound $1.00

HAND SHADOWS TO BE THROWN UPON THE WALL: A SERIES OF NOVEL AND AMUSING FIGURES FORMED BY THE HAND, Henry Bursill. Delightful picturebook from great-grandfather's day shows how to make 18 different hand shadows: a bird that flies, duck that quacks, dog that wags his tail, camel, goose, deer, boy, turtle, etc. Only book of its sort. vi + 33pp. 6½ x 9¼. 21779-5 Paperbound $1.00

WHITTLING AND WOODCARVING, E. J. Tangerman. 18th printing of best book on market. "If you can cut a potato you can carve" toys and puzzles, chains, chessmen, caricatures, masks, frames, woodcut blocks, surface patterns, much more. Information on tools, woods, techniques. Also goes into serious wood sculpture from Middle Ages to present, East and West. 464 photos, figures. x + 293pp.
20965-2 Paperbound $2.00

HISTORY OF PHILOSOPHY, Julián Marías. Possibly the clearest, most easily followed, best planned, most useful one-volume history of philosophy on the market; neither skimpy nor overfull. Full details on system of every major philosopher and dozens of less important thinkers from pre-Socratics up to Existentialism and later. Strong on many European figures usually omitted. Has gone through dozens of editions in Europe. 1966 edition, translated by Stanley Appelbaum and Clarence Strowbridge. xviii + 505pp. 21739-6 Paperbound $3.00

YOGA; A SCIENTIFIC EVALUATION, Kovoor T. Behanan. Scientific but non-technical study of physiological results of yoga exercises; done under auspices of Yale U. Relations to Indian thought, to psychoanalysis, etc. 16 photos. xxiii + 270pp.
20505-3 Paperbound $2.50